The
Joy of
PRAYING THE
PSALMS

The
Joy of
PRAYING THE PSALMS

Nancy Marie de Flon

Resurrection Press
An Imprint of
CATHOLIC BOOK PUBLISHING CORP.
Totowa • New Jersey

All Scripture quotations contained herein except Psalms are from the *New Revised Standard Version Bible:* Catholic Edition, copyright © 1993 and 1989 by the National Council of the Churches of Christ in the U.S.A. Used by permission. All rights reserved.

Psalm quotations, except where indicated are from the *The Psalms, New Catholic Version of the Bible,* copyright © 2002 by Catholic Book Publishing Corp. Used by permission. All rights reserved.

Sources of quotations:

Walter Brueggemann, *Praying the Psalms* (Winona, MN: St. Mary's Press, 1986).

John Eaton, *The Psalms Come Alive* (Downers Grove, IL: Intervarsity Press, 1986).

General Instruction on the Liturgy of the Hours, Liturgy Documentary Series 5, rev. ed. (Washington, DC: USCCB, 2002).

Joseph Gelineau, Introduction, *The Psalms: A New Translation* (Glasgow: Fontana, 1985).

All Vatican documents, including those of the Second Vatican Council, the Wednesday Audiences of the Holy Father, and others can be found on the Vatican website, http://www.vatican.va.

First Published in September, 2005 by
Catholic Book Publishing/Resurrection Press
77 West End Road
Totowa, NJ 07512

© 2005 by Nancy de Flon

ISBN 1-878718-95-9

Library of Congress Catalog Card Number: 2005927390

Cover photo by Nancy Marie de Flon

Cover design by Beth DeNapoli

Printed in the United States of America

1 2 3 4 5 6 7 8 9

www.catholicbookpublishing.com

Table of Contents

DEDICATION

This book is dedicated, with much love and gratitude, to the late Canon Brian Grady (1927-1998), parish priest of Our Lady Queen of Heaven Church, Dovercourt, Essex, England.

Fr. Brian once told me that his favorite psalm verse was "Open wide your mouth, and I will fill it" (Ps 81:11). Perhaps he has fulfilled that by setting me on the long path that has eventually led to this book.

Preface

ONE day many, many years ago I bought a little book of the New Testament and Psalms from a church book rack—not for any particular reason, but only because it seemed to be a good thing to have. Soon afterward, a great crisis arose in my life and I didn't know where to turn. I was pretty panicked. A priest suggested I read Psalm 103, an eloquent meditation on God's love for us.

Later that night I read this beautiful psalm. Within twenty-four hours a feeling of calm came over me and I was able to approach and cope with the situation with greater equanimity than I would ever have thought possible.

That was my introduction to the efficacy of the Psalms in my personal prayer life. Over the years, many dear people have not only helped me pray better but have also helped me develop and clarify my thinking about the Psalms to the point where I could write and offer you this book. First, I want to thank all the students who have attended my parish courses on praying the Psalms, and especially Mrs. Winnie Valcanchik and Msgr. Jim Lisante, who invited me to teach the courses at their parishes on Long Island (St. Agnes Cathedral, Rockville Centre, and St. Thomas the Apostle, West Hempstead, respectively). I am also indebted to my friends Mgsr. Don Hanson and Dr. Joe Collison, who read prehistorically early drafts of my manuscript so long ago that they

probably don't even remember. And without Emilie
Cerar, very dear friend and editor of infinite patience,
this book would *still* never have come to see the light of
day.

Above all, I have to thank Very Rev. Canon Brian
Grady, who first tolerated and encouraged my early
efforts at teaching and writing about the Psalms in our
parish in Dovercourt (Diocese of Brentwood), England. I
only wish he could have lived to see this book's publica-
tion; it's to his memory that it is gratefully and lovingly
dedicated.

Chapter 1

Prayers of a Covenant People

"The God of my ancestors, I praise him"

DO you have a favorite prayer book? I suppose most of us do—it could be a collection of prayers in the tradition of a particular saint, a book of meditations on the rosary, or perhaps an all-purpose "prayers for all occasions." For years I had such a book, bound in red vinyl and with photographs enhancing the texts. Recently, while packing to move to a smaller residence, I decided to give the book away to a friend who I knew would make good use of it. On arriving to begin my new job, what should I find among my predecessor's "left-behinds" but a copy of that same book. God obviously didn't want me to be without it!

Jesus had a favorite prayer book too: it is, and was, the favorite prayer book of all Jewish people. Jesus' prayer book was the Book of Psalms. The Psalms that we know from the Bible originated as the living prayer tradition of the Jewish community.

The Jews aren't a people from whom Christians took over the "true faith" two thousand years ago; rather, they are our ancestors in salvation history. Their prayers, the Psalms, are as much a living part of our salvation family history as the photos we pull out or the stories we retell over and over are a living part of our natural family history. We have a right to own and to experience these prayers just as we own and experience those photos, stories, or other family mementos.

The word *psalm* is originally a Greek word, *psalmos,* which means "a song accompanied by stringed instruments." A psalm is a prayer intended to be sung, and in biblical times the psalm would have been accompanied by instruments such as a lyre or a harp.

How Did the Book of Psalms Come to Be?

Actually, the Book of Psalms is no more "a book" than the Bible itself is "a book." It is a collection of 150 psalms into not one but five smaller books, each of which ends in an exclamation of praise: hence the Hebrew name for the collection in its entirety is *Tehellim* or "Praises." Psalms 41, 72, 89, and 106, which conclude Books 1, 2, 3, and 4 respectively, each end with variations on the praise formula "Blessed be the Lord God of Israel for ever and ever," while Psalm 150—and thereby the entire Book of Psalms—culminates in the great exhortation, "Let everything that has breath praise the Lord!" The larger compilation of these five books into the final Book of Psalms was possibly made for liturgical purposes.

To understand how this collection of psalms was compiled, think of the hymn book you use at church. Perhaps your parish subscribes to a Missalette that gets replaced once or twice a year, or perhaps you are fortunate enough to worship in a parish that uses one of the high-quality permanent worship books. Either way, the hymns and songs in it were compiled by editors who gathered in vast amounts of material and then had to make judgment calls: Is this old standard hymn still sung? Is its theology up to date? What about these more recent hymns and songs—are they still popular? And these new ones: Do they make the grade? Are they singable? Are they what we need right now? Is it worth replacing some of the older material with them?

And for every parish, school, or prayer group that has bought any given hymnal or song book, I can guarantee that at least one person has leafed through it and asked, "Oh, why didn't they include . . . ?"

The same is true of the Book of Psalms. There must have been any number of psalms that weren't included. Some of them, as we'll see, made their way into another part of the Bible.

Here is another parallel with our hymn book: The hymns and songs in it were composed over a long period of time ranging from the chorales of Martin Luther and J.S. Bach to the latest compositions of Michael Joncas and David Haas. So, too, although the compilation of the Old Testament psalms was completed by the third century B.C., the individual psalms were composed by many different people, over a period of several hundred years.

But what about King David? Didn't he compose the Psalms? You can be forgiven for thinking he did, because a tradition already well established by the time of Jesus credits David, who lived around 1000 B.C., with authorship of the Psalms, and the Hebrew Scriptures indeed testify to his poetical and musical gifts: the second Book of Samuel, for example, calls him the "sweet psalmist of Israel" (2 Sam 23:1, RSV).

King David, however, could not have composed all of the psalms. Some of them refer to events that took place long after he lived. Think, for example, of Psalm 137, "By the rivers of Babylon," the desolate cry that the Jewish exiles in Babylon sent up to the Lord some 400 years after David! Nor did he necessarily compose each and every psalm that bears the heading "A Psalm of David"; perhaps many of these were those psalms—his favorites—with which he became associated as performer, or which he was known to have prayed at specific, crucial times in his life. A good example of the latter is the great psalm of repentance, Psalm 51, which he is said to have prayed after he sinned with Bathsheba.

While David was undoubtedly a gifted musician and poet and thus did compose some of the psalms, we now believe his major role in their development to have been that of founder of the psalm tradition itself. It was David who created the environment in which the art of the Psalms flourished, by establishing Jerusalem as the center of worship for the nation of Israel. This spurred the development and organization of forms of worship—liturgies—and for this purpose David founded special guilds of psalmists whose members came from families that devoted their lives to composing and performing for musical worship.

Scripture describes how David "set apart for the service certain of the sons of Asaph, and of Heman, and of Jeduthun, who should prophesy with lyres, harps, and cymbals. . . . They and their kindred, who were trained in singing to the Lord, all of whom were skillful, numbered two hundred eighty-eight" (1 Chr 25:1, 7).

It conjures up visions of a massive cathedral choir school with a gifted and charismatic leader at its head, or an ancient form of the medieval Mastersingers! The memory of the psalmists' guild survives in the brief headings that precede many of the psalms in the Old Testament book: for example, Psalm 42, among others, is attributed to the "sons of Korah," Psalms 73-83 to Asaph, and so forth. David's outstanding contribution to the development of the Psalms, then, was the establishment and organization of the tradition of psalm composing and performing as a stable, permanent feature in Jewish worship. Following David, his royal successors continued to encourage the composing and performing of psalms.

Much later, after the Babylonian Captivity that inspired Psalm 137, the temple and the city of Jerusalem were restored and rebuilt, and possibly the latest of the entries in the Book of Psalms date from the end of this period, around the middle of the fifth century B.C. Thus we have a span of five hundred or more years over which the oldest and most recent Old Testament Psalms were composed.

How Were the Psalms Used?

It cannot be sufficiently emphasized: the Psalms were sung. They were sung in the presence of God, in the Temple, God's "sanctuary" as the Psalms call it. References to music—to instruments as well as to singing—abound in the Psalms. The psalmists praised God with the ten-stringed lyre and the lute (Ps 92:4), the harp (Ps 108), and even, in Psalm 150, an entire orchestra! In his reflection on this psalm Pope John Paul II stressed its musicality, comparing it to the Hallelujah Chorus in Handel's *Messiah*.

The First Book of Chronicles (15:16-24), relating how the Israelites brought the ark up to Jerusalem, records that David commanded the heads of the Levites to apportion the musical duties among their kinsmen: the instruments for which they were responsible included harps, lyres, cymbals and trumpets. And a comparison of the list of instruments in Psalm 150 with those with which David and the Israelites "made merry before the Lord with all their might" (2 Sam 6) makes it clear—the musical allusions in the Psalms are no mere figures of speech. The promise is made, the invitation extended, to take up these instruments in praise because they were the instruments the people had and that they actually used in worship.

Just as we might sing a given hymn in different forms of worship—the Eucharist, for example, or Evening Prayer or Benediction—so, too, the Psalms could be used in a variety of liturgical forms that were celebrated in the

Temple. First there was the routine day-to-day worship in which an individual might come, perhaps with his family or friends, to present a petition or offer thanksgiving. Then, events affecting the community as a whole were occasions for the people to gather in the Temple for praise or for lament. And finally the great seasonal festivals were celebrated: the Feast of Unleavened Bread or the Passover; the Festival of Weeks or Pentecost, which was really a harvest festival; and a major holy season in the autumn, the predecessor to the modern Jewish New Year. This last was the most important festival of the year; John Eaton describes it in *The Psalms Come Alive:*

It was a tremendous occasion. The hillsides around the fortress-city, covered with camps of the pilgrims, resounded with the psalms and acclamations. The sacred way up to the city and temple was the scene of exciting processions. The temple itself, with its bronze pillars and honey-colored stone, gleamed on the summit in the fiery sun. And above all, the people participated with all their hearts. (p. 5)

It is helpful if we can visualize the physical setting in which the people of Israel worshiped their God, for many aspects of it are reflected in the language of the Psalms. As Eaton's description suggests, David's Jerusalem was built on a steep hill. Such a location offers its inhabitants considerable security and protection, and it was natural that this fortress-like town—with the Temple as its summit—became identified as God's stronghold. The Psalms often employ this "fortress" imagery to describe God's steadfast protection:

> For you are my refuge,
> a tower of strength against the enemy. (Ps 61:4)

> He alone is my rock and my salvation,
> my fortress, so that I stand ever unshaken. (Ps 62:3)

Processions were an exciting feature of worship during the major feasts, with the huge throngs of people winding their way like a great snake up the slopes to the Temple wherein dwelled the holy of holies, the ark, the home of the Supreme God. The term "Song of Ascents" at the head of many psalms appropriately indicates those songs that would have accompanied such processions, and the words of many psalms make frequent use of "ascending" language:

> Jerusalem is built as a city
> that is firmly bound together in unity.
> There the tribes go up,
> the tribes of the LORD. (Ps 122:3-4a)

One such psalm familiar to all Christians is Psalm 47, which has long held a place of prominence in our Ascension Day liturgy:

> God has ascended amid shouts of joy;
> the LORD, amid the sound of trumpets. (Ps 47:6)

The language of the Psalms, then, is rooted in concrete experience. The people who performed Psalm 150 in their liturgy really did praise God with the trumpet and the cymbal and in dancing; and, to the accompaniment of the exuberant words and tune of Psalm 47, God literally did "go up"—up the mountain in the ark of the covenant to the Temple.

Many ancient peoples believed music to be a divinely inspired art, and the Jews were no exception. But what is unique about the Jewish tradition is that the source of inspiration was not some muse, not one god among several, but *the* God who loves his people and who, out of this love, initiates a dialogue with them. That dialogue is facilitated by the Psalms, in whose language God and the individual speak to each other.

The Psalms as Prayers of Jesus and His Friends

As a devout Jew, Jesus prayed the Psalms. They were as deeply integral a part of Jesus' prayer life as the Our Father and Hail Mary are to ours. Just as we learned these prayers as a child, so, too, Mary and Joseph taught young Jesus to pray the Psalms. I already mentioned that Scripture contains psalms elsewhere than in the Book of Psalms; two of them are in the NT, and they are the prayers of Jesus' relatives. Did you know that Mary's *Magnificat* (Lk 1:46-55) is a psalm? Compare it with Hannah's song—a psalm preserved in the Hebrew Scriptures in the first Book of Samuel (2:1-10)—and you can see clearly how steeped in the psalm tradition Mary was. Both psalms celebrate the birth of a child who, in the normal course of things, ought not to have been born: Jesus because Mary had had no relations with a man, Samuel because Hannah had been barren for many years. Both psalms exult in a God who turns the world upside down: the strong are made weak and vice versa; the hungry are fed while the rich must labor; the lowly are raised up. What's different about Mary's psalm is its strongly personal nature, her sense of her own place in God's reversal of the usual order: the Almighty has done great things for *me,* God's lowly handmaid.

The other NT psalm is also found in Luke (1:68-79), who puts into the mouth of Zechariah, the father of John the Baptizer, the well-known "Benedictus" canticle, "Blessed be the Lord, the God of Israel." Prayed by Zechariah after the birth and naming of his son, this canticle celebrates how God in his steadfast love has kept the age-old promise of redemption, made through the prophets, by "raising up for us a mighty Savior."

The Psalms came naturally to Jesus as prayer and as material for meditation. In the Gospels we read instances of Jesus quoting from a psalm to illustrate a point for his listeners (for example, Luke 20:42), and the Gospels of Matthew (26:30) and Mark (14:26) mention Jesus and his friends singing psalms at the Last Supper, undoubtedly the so-called Hallel psalms—Psalm 114 through 118 traditionally sung at the end of the Passover meal.

Most poignantly, Jesus came to regard the Psalms, along with other passages in the Hebrew Scriptures, as prophecies about himself. In the Gospel of John Jesus quotes Psalm 41:10 as if it applied directly to himself: "Even my friend whom I trusted, the one who dined at my table, has risen up against me" foretells Judas' betrayal. Luke's Gospel cites two post-resurrection appearances of Jesus in which he explains how all that came to pass regarding Jesus' passion and death was a fulfillment of Scripture. To the disciples en route to Emmaus, perplexed and disappointed at having their hopes about Jesus seemingly dashed, "beginning with Moses and all the prophets, he interpreted to them all the things about himself in all the scriptures" (Lk 24:27). Appearing later in the midst of his disciples, Jesus reminded them of what he said when he was still with them, that "everything written about me in the law of Moses, the prophets, and the psalms must be fulfilled" (Lk 24:44). We can only imagine how it must have been for Jesus to experience a growing awareness of his inevitable fate, when in the course of his life there gradually dawned on him the full import of the prophecies and how they were to be fulfilled. The Gospels record how Jesus foresaw his rejection by his own people. In the Synoptic Gospels (Mt 21:42, Mk 12:10-11, Lk 20:17) Jesus applies verse 22 from Psalm 118, the great victory song, to himself: "The stone the builders rejected has become the cornerstone." Later, the Acts of the Apostles tells how Peter, under arrest for preaching about Jesus and for healing a lame beggar in his name, makes the same association by quoting this verse while addressing the high priest and elders:

"Rulers of the people and elders, . . . let it be known to all of you, and to all the people of Israel, that this man is standing before you in good health by the name of Jesus Christ of Nazareth, whom you crucified, whom God raised from the dead. This Jesus is

'the stone that was rejected by you, the builders;
it has become the cornerstone.' " (Acts 4:8b, 10-11)

The Psalms in the Early Christian Tradition

Just as the Psalms were integral to the prayer life of
the Jews of biblical times and, thus, to Jesus, so, too, were
they equally important to the early Christians, who were
Jews steeped in the Psalm tradition. The various Letters
in the New Testament abound with Psalm references. St.
Paul, especially, enjoined the members of his communities to encourage one another and praise God by singing
"psalms and hymns and spiritual songs" (Eph 5:18-20,
Col 3:16)—note the emphasis on singing!

New Testament authors derived from the Psalms
imagery with which to speak of Christ. When St. Paul
says that Christ "must reign until he has put all enemies
under his feet" (1 Cor 15:25), he is echoing the great messianic Psalm 110: "Sit at my right hand, till I make your
enemies your footstool" (v. 1). And Matthew, conveying
the awesomeness of the voice speaking from heaven
when Jesus emerges from the waters of baptism, appro-
priates the image from Psalm 29:3,

The voice of the Lord echoes over the waters . . .
The Lord thunders over mighty waters.

Given the nature of his audience, the author of that
sublime piece of New Testament writing, the Letter to the
Hebrews, could easily appropriate psalmic language and
imagery to drive home his message that Christ is the messiah, the one to whom his readers owe their allegiance
and faith. He shows how the great messianic psalms 2

and 110 apply to Christ (see, e.g., Heb 1:5, 5:5, 5:6, and chap. 7, which is an extended meditation on Christ as the new "high priest in the line of Melchizedek"); adopts the challenge issued in Psalm 95, "If today you hear his voice, harden not your hearts" (vv. 7c-8a; see Heb chaps. 3 and 4) to exhort his readers to belief in Christ; claims that Psalm 8 testifies to Christ's exalted position at the head of humanity (vv. 4-6; see Heb 2:6-9); and puts into Christ's mouth the words from Psalm 40—"Here I am Lord . . . I come to do your will"—to portray him as a willing high priest (vv. 6-7; see Heb 10:5-7).

During the earliest Christian decades and beyond, the Psalms attained increased significance when they came to be interpreted as messianic prophecies about Jesus. The early Christians, including the authors of the New Testament writings, regarded the Hebrew Scriptures in terms of faith lived from a post-resurrection perspective, faith that acclaims Jesus as the risen Lord, the long-awaited one sent by God. Both St. Peter and St. Paul use the language of Psalm 16—a psalm that blesses the Lord for "not letting his loved one know decay"—to proclaim how God rescued Jesus from death and raised him up (Acts 2:25-28, Peter, on the day of Pentecost, addresses the huge crowd of Jews in Jerusalem; Acts 13:35, Paul addresses the synagogue at Antioch).

Perhaps most importantly, the Gospels quote or allude to the Psalms in reference to the events of Jesus' passion. A verse from Psalm 118, well known to us from our liturgy, figures in all four Gospel accounts of Jesus' triumphant entry into Jerusalem on the first Palm Sunday, when the people greet him with the shout, "Blessed is he who comes in the name of the Lord!" (Mt 21:9, Mk 11:9, Lk 20:38, Jn 12:13; cf. Ps 118:26).

Psalm 22 is often referred to as the great "passion psalm" because of the many allusions to it that are found in the passion accounts. In Matthew's Gospel Jesus uses the opening words of this psalm—"My God, my God, why have you forsaken me?"—on the cross, to express his feeling of abandonment by his Father (27:45). Matthew also alludes to this psalm to show how the onlookers were mocking Jesus: "He trusts in God; let God deliver him now, if he wants to" (Mt 27:43; cf. Ps 22:9).

All four Gospels (Mt 27:36, Mk 15:24, Lk 23:34, Jn 19:34) allude to verse 19 of this psalm: "They divide my garments among them, and for my clothing they cast lots" to depict the soldiers bargaining for Jesus' clothes after crucifying him. Both here and in 19:28, where Jesus says, "I am thirsty" (cf. Ps 22:15), John directly quotes from the psalm and then makes a point of showing how the Scriptures are being fulfilled. It should be noted that this great psalm that opens in searing pain and despair ends on a note of hope and trust; thus even the apparent failure and abandonment that Jesus suffered on the cross would give way to triumph.

Verse 22 of Psalm 69, another great psalm of suffering, ". . . in my thirst they gave me vinegar to drink" is alluded to in all four passion accounts (Mt 27:34, Mk 15:36, Lk

23:36, Jn 19:29), as they describe the soldiers giving Jesus vinegar or sour wine to drink on the cross. And it is from Psalm 31 that Luke takes Jesus' last words, "Into your hands I commend my spirit" (Lk 23:46; cf. Ps 31:5).

It is ironic that so many psalm references in the New Testament should touch precisely on that aspect of Jesus' life which was most absurd and most difficult to accept—his passion. Before the time of Jesus it was not expected that the Messiah, the Savior, would meet such an ignominious end. What had been considered the truly prophetic psalms were those known as the messianic psalms—Psalms 2, 72, and 110—which sing of victory for God's anointed one. Only after Jesus' resurrection were the psalms that describe pathetic suffering associated with his life and death.

The New Testament authors and the huge body of oral and written tradition from which they drew must have had a keen sense of Jesus as human. J.D. Crichton, the great authority on early liturgy, has pointed out that the church uses some psalms in its Holy Week liturgy in such a way as to suggest the interior sentiments of Christ. Early Roman liturgy, he says, was able to "accept without hesitation a depth of humanness in the suffering of Christ that some even today might think excessive. This interpretation is so prevalent in the liturgy of the time that it can be said to have been an authentic expression of the mind of the Church. If this is true, it means we have an insight into the interior sentiments of Christ in his passion of which the Gospels say very little."

Thus, not only do the Gospels afford some insights into the mental suffering of Jesus, but also a tradition developed parallel with the Gospels that probe still more deeply into his experience of his passion.

The Psalms, therefore, provide an invaluable service in giving the Christian tradition the concepts and language for thinking about the humanity of Jesus. As the twentieth-century Jesuit theologian Karl Rahner has noted, there still exists a tendency for people to think somewhat heretically about Christ. The heresy is called Docetism—from the Greek word *Dokein,* meaning "to appear"—and is an early heresy that held that Jesus only *appeared* to be human; he went through the motions but did not really suffer or have human feelings. Yet, the Gospel writers took these psalms that depict intense suffering and associated them with the paschal event. These authors were aware of these psalms not as texts composed by someone who chiefly intended to foretell someone else's fate, but as prayers written by someone who actually found themselves in a situation in which they experienced these feelings. These psalms spring from the depths of human experience. This is where the Psalms become Christian prayer: in the connection between the original human experience from which they sprang and the application of that experience to Jesus, because this implies, in the most telling way, that Jesus shared the human condition in all its tears, sorrows, yearnings, passion, and joys. Jesus tasted the sweetness and the bitterness of human existence.

The Psalms and the Fathers of the Church

The tradition of interpreting the Psalms in the context of Jesus' life, death, and resurrection continued through the early centuries of Christianity and became enshrined in the writings of the Fathers of the Church. These early Fathers, who lived and worked in the East as well as the West, carried on and developed the apostolic tradition in the early centuries of the church. Their writings took many forms and they used a great variety of approaches to interpret Christian teachings. In their efforts to explain the connections between the Hebrew Scriptures and the New Testament, they often employed allegory and typology, in which a person or event from the Hebrew Scriptures was interpreted as a prefigurement, or "type," of Jesus or something relating to his life, death, and resurrection.

The church places some of the typological references from the Fathers at the heads of certain psalms in the Liturgy of the Hours (see chapter 4). This serves as a constant reminder to us of Jesus as the fulfillment of the hopes and desires of the people of the Hebrew Scriptures.

Some of the Fathers interpreted the Psalms in the light of Jesus' incarnation. St. Athanasius, the great third-century Bishop of Alexandria, was one of the foremost authors on the Incarnation and the author of a lengthy letter explaining the Psalms and advising them how to pray them. This *Letter to Marcellinus,* written to a man who was possibly a deacon in the church at Alexandria, has as its overarching theme the two main senses of the Psalms: Christ is Lord of the Psalter, and the words of the Psalms are our own when we want to express our emotions in prayer. Athanasius claimed that Psalm 98, which proclaims that "All the ends of the earth have seen the salvation by our God," "tells of the first coming of the Lord," for he has brought salvation by his coming among us on earth. Athanasius also uses Psalm 99 to praise Christ as "higher than the Cherubim," for Christ redeemed the fallen earth by taking on human nature. According to the third-century Eastern theologian Origen, Psalm 85 celebrates the fact that Christ's coming on earth meant that God blessed the land; truth, as St. Augustine interprets this psalm, is sprung out of the earth in the person of Christ, born of a virgin. The notion that the Incarnation makes creation holy is a bedrock principle of ecotheology.

Not surprisingly, several psalm interpretations by the early Fathers highlight their relationship to Christ's passion and his victorious resurrection. In Psalm 21, a so-called royal psalm that expresses thanksgiving for the king's victory, St. Irenaeus, the second-century bishop of Lyons, discerns Jesus as the king to whom God has given saving help by raising him from the dead. Irenaeus also gives a christological turn to the phrase in Psalm 24, "Lift up your head, O ye gates . . . that the king of glory may come in," envisioning these gates of heaven being opened for Christ "because he was lifted up in the flesh," that is, on the cross.

In Psalm 57 the psalmist, beset by foes bent on destroying him, is nonetheless steadfastly confident in God's saving love. St. Augustine, the great Western theologian and Bishop of Hippo, maintains that this poignant psalm of affliction "celebrates the passion of Christ." Psalm 142 is another psalm of utter reliance on God when the psalmist is being pursued by those who would trap him; St. Hilary, the fourth-century Bishop of Poitiers, asserts that this was "fulfilled by the Lord at the time of his passion." At least two psalms of praise are interpreted as the risen Christ's song of victory: the monastic writer John Cassian (ca.360—ca.435) sees Psalm 30, which praises God for rescuing the psalmist and not letting his enemies triumph, as Christ's song of thanksgiving to his Father after his resurrection, and for St. Athanasius, Psalm 100 becomes Christ's invitation for "those he has redeemed to sing a hymn of victory."

We would be doing the Fathers an injustice, however, if we were to think that in applying some of the psalms to Christ's passion they regarded them *only* as types or prophecies. Rather, the Fathers understood that the human suffering expressed in the Psalms, and to which no one is immune, was drawn up into Christ's passion and somehow made his own; by taking upon himself the human condition in all its brokenness Christ has transformed our suffering. As the Letter to the Hebrews points out:

> Since, therefore, the children share flesh and blood,
> he himself likewise shared the same things, so that

through death he might destroy the one who has the power of death, that is, the devil. . . . Therefore he had to become like his brothers and sisters in every respect, so that he might be a merciful and faithful high priest in the service of God, to make a sacrifice of atonement for the sins of the people. Because he himself was tested by what he suffered, he is able to help those who are being tested.

(Heb 2:14, 17-18)

This is the source of all our hope. Indeed, it is the deepest meaning of the Incarnation, and our most compelling motivation for praying Jesus' prayers, the Psalms, both in public—when we gather to worship as God's people—and in private—when we "go into [our] room and shut the door and pray to [our] Father who is in secret" (Mt 6:6).

Chapter 2

The Psalms as
All-Purpose Prayer

"Pour out your hearts before him"

ARE you looking for words of encouragement for a friend who's going through a bad time? or a suitable expression of apology to a loved one when things have gone wrong? or, how about cheerful birthday wishes for a child? No need to worry—the greeting card industry ensures you a never-failing supply of appropriate sentiments for these and any other occasion you can think of.

But what about when the person you want to communicate with is God? Again, never fear! You can find the right words for every conceivable situation in one of the 150 Psalms.

As prayer, the Psalms are direct. They describe every possible situation, express the entire range of human emotions—whether confidence in God's love or seething rage at an unjust fate—with no holds barred.

The Psalms are inspired prayer. In his Letter to the Romans St. Paul tells us, ". . . the Spirit helps us in our weakness; for we do not know how to pray as we ought, but that very Spirit intercedes with sighs too deep for words" (8:26). We believe that the Bible, and therefore the

Psalms, are the inspired word of God. As Pope John Paul II told us, Christians who pray the Psalms feel "a sort of harmony between the Spirit present in the Scriptures" and the Spirit who dwells within them through their baptism. The Holy Spirit moved the psalmists to utter their words, because God wanted, through the medium of the Psalms, to initiate a dialogue with us. God has initiated this dialogue because God wants to help us. God wants to nurture our growth and development; to help us work out our feelings in prayer; to confirm us in our faith in God's goodness, in the certainty that God is a never-failing source of strength. All this is possible in the two-way communication we call prayer.

The Psalms also assure us that there is no limit to what we can tell God. It's OK to be angry with God; OK to pour forth our perplexity and frustration. As a wise and holy priest once told me, God doesn't want us to act like cardboard cut-outs of how we *think* we should pray. God wants us to be *ourselves* when we pray; God can handle it all!

Why does God invite us to such utter honesty? Because if we hope to grow in our relationship with God—which is the same as progressing toward that "life to the fullest" that Jesus came to bring us—then we must be open and honest with God about our feelings. Embedded in Psalm 32 is a profound psychological truth: "Happy are they whose transgression is forgiven." The psalmist describes the physical symptoms that resulted when at first he refused to acknowledge his sin: ". . . my body wasted away . . . my strength withered steadily as though consumed by the summer heat" (vv. 3a, 4b).

But then he decides to confess his sin to the Lord, and he feels relief at getting it out into the open and experiencing God's forgiveness. Thus, being honest with ourselves and with God confers physical and psychological benefits; we can open ourselves to God's healing only when we acknowledge before God our weaknesses and shortcomings, indeed anything that troubles us.

We may not be comfortable about some of our feelings and may even have difficulty in acknowledging them to ourselves. We go through a sometimes elaborate process of denial because we judge certain feelings to be bad, shameful, impolite, and so forth. The fact is, however, that feelings are morally neutral. They are neither good nor bad in themselves. It is only when we act upon our feelings that we enter the moral realm. Psalm 4 cautions us, "Be angry, but do not sin." St. Paul borrows this verse in his Letter to the Ephesians when he exhorts his readers to good behavior. In other words, it's all right to be angry, but don't let your anger be carried over into action; that's when it becomes sinful.

Once we can accept that God is not going to judge us about our feelings, we should find it easier to be open with God about them. And only if we are open and honest with God can God move in to help us. If we have a pain somewhere in our body but we're unwilling to remove an article of clothing so that the doctor can examine the spot, then the doctor cannot help us. Or if we have a problem with drugs or mental illness but insist on living in a state of denial about it, then again, we can't be helped. Recall that one of the first steps in the Twelve-Step program is admitting that we are powerless over this particular force.

So it is when we talk to God. Whatever the situation is, however horrible or shameful it may seem to us, once we admit it in prayer, then God can step in and begin working on it with us. The Psalms even invite us to this attitude of honesty. Psalm 62 enjoins us, "Pour out your hearts before him." The author of the Letters of Peter takes up this same theme: "Unload your worries unto God since he is looking after you."

Whether we wish to express joy at good fortune, sorrow for sin, distress over pain, or anger with an enemy, the Psalms cover the entire range of human emotions. They leave no personal experience untouched as material for prayer, and they provide us with ready-made models for communicating with God. If we're at a loss for prayer-words, the Psalms give us a script; and if we want to use our own words, the Psalms give us a model. The Psalms encourage us to reflect on our life situation and "pour out" our feelings to God—to a God who has lived on earth and shared these experiences; a God who knows what it is to be overwhelmed by tiredness and anger, to be transported by joy, to feel tender love; a God described in the Letter to the Hebrews as a high priest who has become like us in every way but sin.

God can deal with anything you want to tell him—including being angry with God himself. If we are truthful with God at all times, that truth, as Jesus promised, will set us free and lead, in turn, to the object of the entire exercise, which is inner healing. God wants to bring us to wholeness, and as soon as we, too, want this wholeness and acknowledge to God our need of and desire for it, then God's grace can flow freely in our lives.

Prayer Themes in the Psalms

Here let us look at the general moods, themes, and situations expressed in the Psalms. You may wish first to read this section through with your Bible or Psalm book handy, and if one of these themes particularly appeals to you, you can look up a suggested psalm straight away. Sometimes you may wish to pray a psalm that acts as a counterbalance to a situation rather than one that directly focuses on and expresses your mood. For example, you may wish to pray a psalm of confidence in God's loving care not only when you are completely at peace and basking in awareness of God's love for you, but also when you are in great distress and need that reminder that God is looking after you in all situations and that you are safe in God's hands.

First, two things should be noted. You will notice that some psalms appear in more than one category. Psalm 6, for example, is a psalm of repentance, but it can also be prayed to express general distress; Psalm 92 is both a thanksgiving psalm and a meditation on God's goodness, compassion, and love. The overlapping tells us that the Psalms are too rich to be narrowed down to one specific theme. This is part of the beauty of the Psalms; each one is like a jewel that flashes different rays of light depending on which way you turn it. So, please don't think of these prayer themes as a rigid classification of the Psalms, but rather as general ideas to help you get started making friends with psalms that can have personal meaning for you.

Also, you won't find all 150 Psalms listed under the prayer themes. I invite you to read prayerfully through all the Psalms—not all at once, but perhaps one or two or three at a time, to discover for yourself how these living expressions of human thoughts and feelings speak *to* you and how you can let them speak *for* you to God. I guarantee that you will be rewarded with a priceless treasury of new prayer-friends.

Praise and worship

Most of the "praise" psalms will help us to praise God as Lord of creation and joyfully to acknowledge God's care of creation. Psalm 104 is a lengthy paean of praise to God whose creative Spirit continuously gives life to the world, while the great hymns that end the Book of Psalms—147 to 150—invoke all creation to join in acclaiming God as mighty and faithful Lord. Other psalms praise the Lord as our Savior (95 and 98), as shepherd of his flock (95 and 100), or as a God both compassionate and mighty (113 and 117). Many of these psalms were undoubtedly intended to be sung by the entire community; we can easily imagine the people, assembled for worship, ringing out the recurring refrain of Psalm 136—"for his love endures for ever"—to each verse sung by the cantor. Yet, they are equally suited to our individual prayer.

The ancient peoples associated the mountains and seas with great power and might, and Psalms 65 and 95 acclaim God as Lord over these natural forces. Psalms 105, 135, and 136 praise God's faithfulness to his people by singing of the many instances of God's saving intervention in Israel's history.

Psalms 8 and 19 are especially fruitful for meditating upon the marvels of God's creation and our place in it. Israel's worship of God as King provides material for Psalm 47—familiar from our Ascension Day liturgy with its verse, "God goes up with shouts of joy"—and for Psalms 48, 96, and 97.

Thanksgiving

The three prayer motifs that run through the psalms of thanksgiving can serve as good prayer models for our own personal relationship with God. *First,* we respond to God's favor to us by witnessing to God's goodness: we tell everyone of God's favors. *Second,* we respond in this way because we have promised to do so. When we prayed for God's help we promised to declare God's goodness to all once our prayer had been heard. *Third,* God is our constant, trustworthy refuge and help in time of trouble. God has helped us before and will continue always to help us.

Psalm 116 is a straightforward example of this type of psalm. It starts by stating the reason for the praise: "I love the Lord because he has heard the cry of my voice."

I called on God and God came to my assistance. I will repay the Lord's goodness by offering praise before all the people. This is what I promised to do, and by praying this psalm I am fulfilling that promise.

Psalm 18, attributed to King David after his many military victories, thanks God in epic proportions. Rich in metaphor and exuberant in its praise, it is an excellent prayer for anyone wishing to thank God for rescue from trouble. Psalm 138, which thanks our kind and faithful God for hearing our prayer, is used as a Responsorial Psalm in our Thanksgiving Day liturgy. *Other psalms: 30, 66, 92, 107, 118.*

God's goodness, compassion, and love

Some of these are thanksgiving psalms that particularly emphasize God's love and care for the individual soul. Psalm 103—"Bless the Lord, O my soul"—is an especially beautiful example, as are Psalms 145 and 146. Psalm 34 is often used in our liturgy in a eucharistic context: "Taste and see that the Lord is good." We may wish to pray such a psalm not only when we are moved to thank God for a specific manifestation of goodness but, even more importantly, when we are down and burdened by our own weakness, and thus need reminding that God is our refuge, our healer, the fount of mercy. *Other psalms: 92, 111.*

Other psalms of this type have confidence in God as their theme and help us to find comfort or strength in God's love. Psalm 23—"The Lord is my shepherd"—is the most familiar of these. Psalm 27 trusts in God to grant a moral victory, while Psalms 16 and 131 are the ultimate declarations of unwavering trust in God as a source of peace. Psalms 31 and 56 express confidence at times of distress. *Other psalms: 26, 46, 62, 121, 125.*

General distress

Too often our prayers of petition may resemble a litany of "wants" in which we treat God as a Santa Claus ever ready to hand out goodies for the asking. Like the thanksgiving psalms, the psalms of distress have recurrent elements associated with requesting God's favor and promising thanks. These psalms provide good models of petitionary prayers that assist us in focusing on and expressing our faith and hope in a God who cares for us.

The first element is that we remember God's help in the past. We remind God that he has helped us before, and this gives us the confidence and courage to ask for God's help again.

Second, we express our complete confidence that God will come to our aid. So confident are we that we promise to praise and thank God for hearing our prayer. In fact, we promise to thank God publicly, "in the great assembly," and thereby become a living testimony to God's love.

The model par excellence of this kind of psalm is Psalm 22, which Jesus prayed on the cross: "My God, my God, why have you abandoned me?" Sometimes we mistakenly think this psalm to be a prayer of unrelieved desolation, and yet it is a prayer of distress and petition in the true psalm tradition: in praying this poignant psalm we relate our present distress, recall God's help to us in the past, ask God's help in our present trouble, and, finally, promise to praise God when our prayer has been answered.

Psalms 6 and 13 both share this pronounced mood of hope and anticipation, while Psalm 142 forthrightly declares our faith by taking for granted that God will help: "Set me free from my prison, so that I may praise your name"—not "*If* you set my free from my prison." The strongly graphic Psalm 69, another "Passion psalm" because lines from it have been applied to Jesus' suffering on the cross, employs the imagery of drowning to depict our distress; yet it also expresses our trust in God's help and a promise that "the poor when they see it will be glad."

Repentance

The psalms of repentance are among the most valuable of all psalms because they teach us the true nature of repentance and of the relationship between God and the penitent. These psalms correct any notion we may have of God as an arbitrary lawmaker who punishes us when we disobey and who exacts (unrealistic!) promises from us never to sin again. Instead, they reveal a God who wants us to be open and honest with him so that he can teach us his ways and let us be guided by the Spirit who is the source of wisdom.

Psalm 32, as already mentioned, teaches the benefits of being honest with God. Psalm 51 is the penitential psalm par excellence:

> Have mercy on me, God, in your kindness;
> in your compassion blot out my offense.

According to tradition, King David composed this psalm after the prophet Nathan rebuked him for his adultery with Bathsheba. The church prays this psalm throughout the penitential season of Lent: it is the Responsorial Psalm for the Mass on Ash Wednesday and on many other days in Lent, and it is also the first psalm in Morning Prayer each Friday, the day when the church sets before us the memory of Christ's passion and death for our sins.

If we want to beg God's mercy and forgiveness for various sins, we can pray Psalms 6, 102, and 122; and if we wish to express our trust in God's mercy, Psalm 130, with its well-known text "Out of the depths I cry to you, O Lord," will give us the words.

Emptiness, loneliness, darkness of spirit

It's not uncommon for us, when we have troubles, to deny that they exist—to sweep under the carpet our fears, for example, or the experience of being hurt. One predictable way of reacting to these situations is to distract ourselves, perhaps with eating, drinking, or shopping sprees. But then, suddenly or gradually, we realize that we are trying to fill an inner emptiness. And we turn and share it with God, because in the end God is the ultimate object of our longing. That greatest of all seekers, St. Augustine, said it so well: "You have made us for yourself, God, and our hearts are restless until they rest in you." He must have been inspired by the opening words of Psalm 62, an excellent prayer aid at these times: "In God alone is my soul at rest; my help comes from him."

While it's natural for us to want to give direct expression to our feelings in prayer, it can also be good to try a different tack. Staying with our feelings can sometimes result in our getting stuck in them so that we end up wallowing in self-pity. This can be especially true of something like loneliness. When this gets us down we want to take our minds off ourselves and instead keep our minds fixed on God, who consoles and heals us. Psalm 103 is an outstanding example of a counterbalance to feelings and situations of fear, loneliness, or emptiness. It recalls the many ways in which God's goodness comes to us, and thereby gives us the strength to go on. For other psalms of this kind, see *God's goodness, compassion, and love,* above.

Depression

True depression is a physically and mentally debilitating experience that renders the sufferer incapable of concentrating on anything. It seems to isolate the person from his or her surroundings, as if a curtain had been drawn down between the sufferer and the rest of the world. Psalm 88 gives voice to this experience. Honest and direct, it is the only psalm to end on a truly negative note: "Friend and neighbor you have taken from me; my one companion is darkness." The church prays this psalm at Night Prayer each Friday, thereby recalling

Christ's feeling of desolation and abandonment as he hung on the cross.

Communal lament/Disaster

Referred to by biblical scholars as psalms of national lament, these psalms were composed following disasters in Israel's history. When they suffered resounding military defeats, when the temple was ruined and Jerusalem destroyed, the people of Israel felt that God had rejected them and they gave vent to this in prayer. In our own time we, too, are no strangers to large-scale disasters, whether a natural one such as a devastating earthquake on the other side of the world or a human-inflicted event close to home, such as the terrorist attacks on September 11. Aware that the tragedy suffered by our brothers and sisters affects us as well, we can turn to these psalms for support at such times.

Psalm 80, which vividly depicts the ravaged state of God's chosen people and begs God, "stir up your power and come to save us," may well be an appropriate prayer for our church in its time of tribulation. Psalm 85 finds hope by recalling God's past help for his people and expresses confidence that God will once again "revive us" and reverse our fortunes. Psalms 44, 74, and 79 are also intensely graphic psalms of communal lament.

Longing for God

As humans we have an innate yearning for some transcendent reality, something infinitely greater than anything already known to us. As Christians we are fortunate in being able to identify our almighty God and Creator as the object of this yearning. Certain psalms can be valuable prayer aids when we want to express this longing for God. Psalms 42 and 43 are so similar, they may have originally been one psalm. Probably composed during the time of Israel's captivity in Babylon, they give voice to the exile's yearning for the homeland; but any of us who experience deep longing for and openness to God can relate to the exiled Israelites' longing to worship God in the temple in Jerusalem.

The poetic imagery of thirst used in Psalms 42 and 63 is graphic because its basis is biological fact: just as our body cannot survive without water, so, too, our soul depends on God for nourishment. Pope John Paul II has pointed out that the deer that longs for running streams symbolizes the praying person who tends with his or her whole being toward the Lord. *Another psalm: 84.*

Petitions for justice, protection, and strength

Whether we seek God's protection as a constant, abiding presence in our lives or at a specific time when we feel threatened, we can find a wealth of assistance in the psalms for pouring out our hearts before God.

On an occasion when we have been the victim of a crime, the object of gossip, or rejected by someone we have loved, we can pray with the authors of Psalms 7, 17, or 35. Some 2,500 years ago these authors found themselves in such predicaments and were inspired by the Holy Spirit to address these psalms to God, in which they identify themselves as the underdog, persecuted by persons wicked and stronger than they, or unfairly accused by the enemy. Another situation that can over-whelm us with its injustice is when we see the wicked thrive while good people suffer. At such times Psalm 58 provides the prayer-words for us.

Many psalms of this type have an exceedingly angry tone and call upon God to strike our enemy down. To a Christian, making these emotions the stuff of prayer may well seem at odds with our concept of the "proper" things to say when we pray. Yet, this way of praying was a decidedly healthy aspect of the Jewish religious tradi-tion; the Jewish people did not hesitate to vent their feel-ings to God in this way (Psalms 59, 109, and 140 are good examples). Remember what we said earlier about God wanting our openness and honesty: our God is creator and Lord of every part of our being, not just the "good" parts that praise and thank and are polite, and such a God welcomes and even encourages us to pray with our entire being. If it is natural on occasion to experience angry, even violent emotions, then it is also natural, as well as acceptable, to make these emotions the material of our prayer. Yet, even in these psalms, just as in the praise psalms, we promise to praise and thank God for coming to our aid, for even our anger and frustration are tempered by trust in God's loving care.

With other psalms we can call upon God's strength-giving protection to be ever present to us. Psalm 25 appeals to the Lord for protection and asks God to lead and guide us in the truth. The imagery of a parent bird protecting its young occurs frequently in the Psalms, and

Psalm 61 asks God, "Hide me in the shelter of your wings." If we want to find comfort and protection in the knowledge that God searches and knows us intimately, we can do no better than to turn to the beautiful Psalm 139.

Wisdom

By describing the good person—the wise person who trusts in God—and contrasting her or him with the evil person (the foolish person who trusts in her or his own wealth or power), these psalms offer material for reflection on how to seek out and walk God's paths. We might also call them "ways of living" psalms.

The Book of Psalms appropriately begins with a wisdom psalm that contrasts the individual "whose delight is in the law of the Lord" with the wicked whose ways "lead to doom." Its image of the good person as a tree planted near and nourished by streams of water occurs elsewhere in the Bible, notably in the Book of Jeremiah. Psalm 49, with its refrain "In his riches, man lacks wisdom: he is like the beasts that are destroyed" is an extended meditation upon the folly of envy, especially envy of the wealthy. Psalm 37, "Do not fret because of the wicked," can be appreciated as advice from an old and wise person who knows well the ephemeral nature of evil's victory, while the good will prevail in the end. The really ambitious can benefit from Psalm 119: with its 176 verses it's a mini-Book of Wisdom all on its own! Psalm 119 was written in praise of the Torah, or divine Law and Word. Pope John Paul II observed that each of its 176 verses contains at least one of the eight words that are used to define the Torah: law, word, witness, judgment, saying, decree, precept, order. Through this psalm, he said, we celebrate divine revelation itself. *Other psalms: 15, 73, 112.*

The Psalms as a School of Prayer

The Psalms, then, speak for us when we are at a loss for the words to express our feelings to God. But they do more than that: they can also help and inspire us to use our own words—to improvise variations on a theme, as it were, so as to make the prayer truly our own.

In this we can have no better role model than Jesus himself. The Gospel of Mark records that Jesus on the cross cried out the opening words of Psalm 22—"My God, my God, why have you abandoned me?"—but Mark does not go on to tell us how Jesus may have continued this prayer in his heart, with his own words. Could it have been a prayer of perplexity? of disappointment? or perhaps even a prayer of desperate, straw-clutching faith? For this great "passion psalm" is far from being an expression of unremitting desolation but, rather, rallies in the confidence that God will come to the psalmist's aid, giving him reason to render thanks to God in the midst of all the people.

While teaching a course on Praying the Psalms in a parish Adult Religious Education program I once asked the class to compose psalms of their own, and the results were amazingly, truly personal and poetic expressions of the students' innermost feelings. Try it some time, confident that the Spirit will be there to assist you! You don't need the technical mastery of a Coleridge or a Wordsworth—only the desire to communicate openly and honestly with God.

Here is an exercise that may help you get started. Choose a psalm, any psalm that relates generally to the feeling or situation about which you want to speak to God. Prayerfully read through the psalm, asking the Spirit to help you find an appropriate verse. When you find that verse—one that has a special meaning for you—remain with it. Rather, let it remain with you. Keep turning it over, pondering it in your heart, as Mary did with so many things, while God gradually speaks its meaning to you. Use it as a "conversation starter" with God as you go on to say the same thing in your own words and to expand on the original sentiment. When you first attempt this exercise, you can do it for a short period of time, perhaps three or four minutes, but after you become accustomed to praying this way you may wish to increase the amount of time you spend at it.

The flexibility of the Psalms allows us to apply them to a variety of moods and situations, including the desire merely to be with God and let God speak to us. This flexibility springs from the many shades and levels of meaning that can be applied to certain words and expressions. Some psalms, for example, refer to an "enemy," perhaps begging God's protection against the foe or asking God to strike the enemy down. That enemy can be within as well as outside me; it can be another human being, but it may also be a temptation, an illness, or any distressing psychological situation. Psalm 143 is a great example of an all-purpose "enemy" psalm; the psalmist describes a feeling of exhaustion from being pursued by an adversary and implores God's protection. Words such as hunger, thirst, and famine also have double layers of physical and spiritual connotations; and the word *poor* can yield many riches if we think of the reference in the Beatitudes to the "poor in spirit," meaning those who acknowledge their complete dependence on God. As long as we are open to the many possible interpretations of such words and phrases, the Psalms will continue to offer ever richer potential for communication with God.

St. Athanasius, one of the great early Fathers of the Church who lived in the fourth century, is supposed to have commented that "most of Scripture speaks *to* us, while the Psalms speak *for* us." Try praying them frequently, and you will discover that they do both. If we are searching for help in our communication with God, we will hardly find it in a better place than the Book of Psalms.

Chapter 3

The Psalms, Poetry, and Prayer

"Come before him, singing for joy"

"POETRY is the indirect expression in words, most appropriately in metrical words, of some overpowering emotion, or ruling taste, or feeling."

John Keble, the author of this definition of poetry, was an Anglican clergyman, a friend of John Henry (later Cardinal) Newman, and one of the great religious poets of the nineteenth century. His collection of devotional poetry, *The Christian Year,* provided spiritual nourishment for countless families throughout Victorian England and beyond. Keble understood the power of poetry and, most importantly, its power to help us "lift our minds and hearts to God" and its capacity for doing the work of the Holy Spirit by supplying words for us to pray when we cannot find our own words.

Poetry and prayer, then, are inextricably connected. Of no form of prayer is this more true than the Psalms. The Psalms are lyrical prayer; they are poetry intended to be prayed.

The Psalms express feelings; indeed, through their words they often channel overpowering feelings. In chapter 2 we saw how the Psalms help us to "pour out our hearts" to God. The Psalms are *real*—they were not composed according to an imaginary blueprint of how a person "ought" to pray.

In this chapter I want to explain how our understanding of the Psalms as poetry will deepen and enhance our use of them as prayer in our personal lives. I will then also show you how we can make the poetic techniques of the Psalms our own in order to fashion our personal prayers.

The Psalms and Poetic Language

Because the Psalms are poetry they often convey their message in poetic language. In particular, they make use of metaphors.

Webster's Dictionary defines metaphor as "a figure of speech in which a word or phrase literally denoting one kind of object or idea is used in place of another to suggest a likeness or analogy between them"; metaphor, then, is figurative language. Within it we find (1) the actual figure of speech; (2) the thing signified by it. For a metaphor to convey any meaning, it must be rooted in reality: the figure of speech that is used to signify something must be recognized and understood in its natural, everyday context by the group of people by or for whom the metaphor is used. For example, the Temple at Jerusalem was located on a rocky ridge. The association of the holy Temple site with this natural fortress-like quality inspired the people to call God their rock or their stronghold. Thus, the metaphor of *rock, fortress,* or *stronghold* as used in the Hebrew Scriptures to describe God is rooted in the people of Israel's experience of the characteristics of the Temple site; it is not simply a figure of speech that a psalmist made up out of nowhere.

The Psalms contain three kinds of metaphors:

1. metaphors that the original audience—the people of Israel—understood as such. For example, "flood," "watery depths," and similar expressions, which are rooted in the torrential floods that can suddenly end a dry season (see below), are psalmic metaphors for any kind of grave danger.

2. terms or expressions understood literally both by the original audience and by us, the people of the New Covenant, but we understand them in light of Christian revelation. A good example is the "ascending" imagery found in the "Songs of Ascent," as described in chapter 1: in the time of our forebears in the faith, "God-with-us" ascended the slopes of Jerusalem to the Temple in the great processions; we, according to the New Covenant, celebrate Christ's ascension into heaven after his resurrection.

3. terms that are understood literally both by the original audience and by Christians, but that also have the potential to be used metaphorically in our prayer. The psalms that recall the history of God's dealings with the chosen people abound with such terms.

We will consider both kinds of metaphor as we go along, asking ourselves how we can make the psalmic metaphors our own in our personal praying of the Psalms.

It is important to explore this aspect of the Psalms, because being aware of the origin and meaning of their metaphors will shed light on the original meaning of the passages in which they appear. In this way our own praying of the Psalms will be considerably deepened if we can truly enter the minds and hearts of our ancestors in salvation history who composed and prayed them. But more than that, being comfortable with the metaphors will also guide us in applying them to our own experiences and, thus, in allowing them truly to speak to us and for us. This, in turn, will open us to finding in the Psalms our own metaphors that have specific meanings for us. As Scripture scholar Walter Brueggemann points out in *Praying the Psalms*, "The Psalmic metaphors we consider offer to us . . . movements of God that will change things. Praying the Psalms means openness to God's pilgrimage toward us" (p. 40).

Metaphors and Their Meanings

Let us now look at some of the metaphors in the Psalms. A few of them are unfamiliar and exotic place names; others are everyday, ordinary terms such as names of animals and other natural features. After each term the numbers of those psalms in which each one appears is given, so that if you wish, you can first read the explanation of a term and then look it up in the context of the actual psalm or psalms.

Bashan. A high, rich, grain-producing region east of the Sea of Galilee. To the Israelites it was a land of mountains, huge cattle, sheep, lions, oaks, and powerfully

built people. The "strong bulls of Bashan" were legendary, and the people, together with the Amorites, were
among the aboriginal giants who inhabited Canaan and
the surrounding regions. Og, king of Bashan, and Sihon,
king of the Amorites, suffered decisive defeats at the
hands of the Israelites during the conquest of the
Promised Land. Psalm 68 refers to the strength and
power of Bashan, portraying its mighty mountains as
envious because God has made the smaller Mount Zion
the "highest mountain" by choosing it as his dwelling
place. The "bulls of Bashan," by their very nature, would
symbolize an adversary of overpowering strength. The
author of Psalm 22 uses the metaphor of the "fierce bulls
of Bashan" to describe his plight of being surrounded by
foes with no one to help him. *See also Psalms 135 and 136.*

Cedars of Lebanon. Their name itself means
"strength." These trees produced strong, durable, fra-
grant wood, and were much sought after for the construction of public and holy buildings and other important items. They appear in the Psalms as metaphors for
and symbols of physical or moral strength, frequently to
point out the superior strength of the Lord God. In Psalm
29, a very ancient hymn to the sheer elemental might of
the "God of glory," the Lord's voice is powerful enough
to shatter the cedars of Lebanon. The wicked person may
tower like a cedar of Lebanon and yet is no match for the
Lord (Ps 36), while the just person flourishes like a cedar
of Lebanon (Ps 92).

Dogs. In the Bible dogs are not a loving, faithful
domestic pet. Scripture never depicts dogs in a good

light. They are outcasts, scavengers, lazy, stupid, and noisy. "Dog" was an expression of contempt. Psalm 68:24 offers a literal reference to how the Hebrews viewed dogs: "You may bathe your feet in the blood of your foes and the tongues of your dogs have their share." In Psalm 59 the psalmist appeals to God for protection against evil foes, whom he compares to a pack of howling wild dogs roaming the city in search of food.

Flood. In the biblical countries lengthy dry spells are commonly followed by torrential floods. It can be quite dangerous to be caught in the wrong place at the wrong time when these floods come, because they arise very suddenly. In Hebrew poetry "flood" can also and often does refer to the sea. It is a metaphor for overwhelming, inexorable fate. The author of Psalm 69—which, along with Psalm 22, is one of the great psalms considered in the Christian tradition to allude to the passion of Christ—graphically portrays himself as being engulfed and overwhelmed by waves. In Psalm 18, King David's song of victory, God is praised for having snatched the psalmist out of "the mighty waters." Psalm 32 carries the assurance that God will never let the floods of water destroy the good person who prays to God in need.

Lions. In Old Testament times lions were numerous in Palestine. They lurked in the Jordan Valley and the mountains of Judah and Samaria. Thus their presence was always a very real danger or threat to travelers or to anyone who had to be in the mountains. That the shepherd in Psalm 23 guides his sheep along the right path is because in those days a sheep did not have to stray far from the right path to be in real danger from lions. Psalms 17 and 22 compare the enemies surrounding the psalmist with "ravening and roaring lions." Psalm 17, especially, points up the unpredictability of the enemy— one never knows quite when the enemy is about to attack. Psalm 91 depicts the psalmist overcoming his foes: he will trample on the lion. (Note v. 12, the famous line that the devil quotes to Jesus when he tempts Jesus to throw himself from the roof of the Temple.)

Oxen. In biblical times the ox was highly valued for its strength and it was used for heavy labor. Oxen were also apt to gore people, however, so much so that the law prescribed strict consequences for those occasions when one man's ox gored another person. This less desirable quality of oxen figures in Psalm 22, in which the psalmist appeals for protection.

The Pit. The book of Genesis, chapter 37, tells the story of Joseph, the youngest son of Jacob, who was also his favorite. Joseph's brothers, who are all jealous of him, conspire to kill him. But one of the brothers, Reuben, proposes, "Let's not kill him. Instead cast him into this pit here in the wilderness," and so they do, leaving Joseph there to die. To throw someone into the pit is to deny them the resources they need to live; it is to reduce them to powerlessness. **The grave** and **Sheol** have the same meaning. Sheol does not mean "hell" as we conceive it but is, rather, equivalent to the Greek "Hades": the Underworld, a shadowy, silent place where the Hebrews believed the departed spirits went. "The pit," then, is one of the most powerful biblical metaphors for adversaries or an adverse situation. It is a place where you put people in order to remove them from life and even to isolate them from God. In Psalms 6 and 28 communication with God is cut off. Psalm 88, the most pessimistic of the 150 psalms, eloquently describes the inability of souls in the Pit to praise God. What is the cause of the psalmist's desolation? Severe depression? A dread disease? Any number of interpretations suggest themselves.

Several psalms praise God for rescuing the psalmist from the Pit; *see especially Psalms 16, 30, 40, and 86.* A very important, extraordinarily poetic psalm shot through with imagery of being drawn up from the Pit is not in the Book of Psalms at all but in the book of Jonah, chapter 2. Jonah in the belly of the whale is, of course, a well-known "type" of the resurrection of Jesus.

Rock, refuge, stronghold, fortress. King David's Jerusalem was built on a steep hill. Such a location offers its inhabitants considerable security and protection, and it was natural for this fortress-like town, with the Temple at its summit, to become identified as God's stronghold and for God, in turn, to be identified as the people's rock and stronghold or fortress. Psalm 18, David's great psalm of praise to the Lord for saving him from his enemies, acclaims God as "my rock, my fortress, my deliverer. . . . my rock in whom I take refuge, . . . my stronghold" (v. 3).

Psalm 46, which acknowledges God as "our refuge and strength," inspired Martin Luther's great hymn, "A

Mighty Fortress is Our God." *See also Psalms 31, 61, 62, 144.*

Wings. The image of a parent bird protecting its young by taking them under the wing is a common one in Scripture. The Gospels of Matthew and Luke record the words of Jesus when he is lamenting over Jerusalem: "Jerusalem, Jerusalem, how often would I have gathered your children together as a hen gathers her brood under her wings!" In the Hebrew Scriptures, the song of Moses, in the Book of Deuteronomy, that recounts God's dealings with the Hebrews contains a well-known use of "wing" imagery to symbolize God's protection: "Like an eagle that stirs up its nest, that flutters over its young, spreading out its wings, catching them, bearing them on its pinions, the Lord alone did lead him" (Deut 32:11). Combine this with verse 4 from Psalm 91—"you will take refuge under [God's] wings"—and you have the text of the song "On eagle's wings." I once heard the composer of this song, Fr. Michael Joncas, explain how he had been inspired to write it after observing an eagle doing precisely what is described in the above passage from Deuteronomy. Many years ago I worked in an office where, one spring, I was privileged to watch a pair of moorhens build their nest and raise their young in a pond outside my window. One day a heavy rain shower suddenly hit, and immediately all the baby moorhens dashed for cover under their mother's wings. She stood motionless in that one spot protecting her young until the rain had passed. To observe these powerful images in action illustrates the concrete daily life from which the psalmists drew the metaphors for their poetry.

Making the Metaphors Your Own

Walter Bruggemann tells us in *Praying the Psalms*, "Our work in praying the Psalms is somehow to bring *the stylized, disciplined speech* of the Psalms together with the *raw, ragged, mostly formless experience* in our lives" (p. 40). One way to do this is by exploring the metaphors to find in them words we can stretch, words whose applications we can widen, in order to let them resonate with and give expression to our own feelings and experience. It is through these metaphors, above all, that we can allow the Psalms to serve as a prayer-vessel that we can fill with the joys and challenges of our ordinary lives. You don't have to be a poet to be able to use metaphors eloquently and effectively in your prayer! All you need is the desire, in your conversations with God, to give words to the things that overwhelm you, that concern you or make you angry—even the things that bring you joy.

Let us now be open to how we can allow some of the psalmic metaphors to speak to us and for us in our own prayers.

One broad group of metaphors depicts some sort of *adversary*. The adversary could be external—a lost relationship, for example, or a professional crisis—or something within ourselves: a temptation, or unresolved anger toward another person.

When we are confronted with an overpowering foe, *bulls of Bashan* and *lions* are metaphors that can help us put our prayers into words. The lion, in particular, symbolizes an enemy that seemingly lies in wait to take us unawares and swallow us. Perhaps someone—a relative or coworker, for example—is harassing us or conspiring against us and we feel powerless to stop the injustice that threatens us. Or perhaps the foe that overpowers us is within us: for example, virtually uncontrollable emotions of anger or despair. Have you experienced such a situation? How can you use one of these metaphors to verbalize your fears and ask God to deliver you? At the same time, you may also wish to remember Psalm 23 and ask the Lord, your shepherd, to guide you on safe paths.

The metaphors of water engulfing us—*floods, torrents, waves*—are apt prayer metaphors when things get on top of us and threaten to overwhelm us. For example, we may be inundated with demands or deadlines; overloaded with responsibilities; overwhelmed by the events and emotions attendant upon major transitions in our lives (a job change, moving, or divorce, for example). Have you ever had such an experience? How can you bring it to God using one of these "water" metaphors? As a corrective, you may wish to pray with a new "nautical" metaphor—"The Lord is my lifeline"—visualizing yourself hanging on to God for dear life while the waves are buffeting you. Sometimes, though, you may feel, as the psalmist does on occasion, that it is God who is actually sending the waves to engulf you. Do not be afraid to express this in prayer! God accepts anything we have to tell him. Perhaps you might consider turning the "water" metaphor around by recalling, and incorporating into your prayer, water's positive aspects in Psalm 23, for example ("[God] leads me to tranquil streams"), and in the story of Jesus and the Samaritan woman in John's Gospel, in which Jesus promises to give "living water" (John 4:10-14).

One of the most important metaphors for an adversary is that of *the Pit*. In many psalms in which the psalmist begs to be rescued from the Pit, he is praying about being healed of a grave physical illness. The Pit may well still refer to such a situation; it can also be a powerful way of prayerfully describing a relationship with God that has been thrown off kilter. Something about ourselves is not as it should be; we are disoriented. Our enemy is within us, and it eats away at the core of our being as surely as rust corrodes the paint on a shiny new car.

Frequently, the psalmist is in the Pit or on its edge, and God draws the person back. The central event in the Christian tradition in which this happened is the death and resurrection of Christ. We share in this experience when we (or our loved one) have been healed, or when our relationship with God has been restored and we perceive that we are being brought to new life. Our faith-relationship with God doesn't protect us from the Pit, but the power of God brings us out of the Pit—not back to our old life but to new life.

You may wish to bring to prayer the "pits" you have experienced in your own life. Have you experienced your own grave illness or injury, or that of a loved one? Or was it a moral, spiritual, or psychological crisis? How did you pray to God about it? How would you pray about it now that you can use the "Pit" imagery of the Psalms?

Have you ever experienced being rescued by God from the Pit? How did God help you? You might wish to jot down a brief psalm-verse of your own in petition or thanksgiving to God.

Another broad group of psalmic metaphors are those that offer images of God's love, care, and protection.

Who in your life is a *cedar of Lebanon*—a source or icon of strength? A friend? a mentor? God? You may wish to use this beautiful metaphor to thank God for sending you this person and to ask God to bless them, or to praise God for being your strength. Do you enjoy music or like to worship God in song? If so, you can augment your prayer with the sentiment found in Psalm 118:4 and Exodus 15:2—"The Lord is my strength and my song."

When we want to praise God for his steadfast love and care, or when we need prayerfully to remind ourselves of God's never-failing love for us, we may find *rock, refuge, stronghold,* and *fortress* suitable prayer metaphors. When have you experienced God as your rock, your stronghold or refuge? How did God play this role in your life at that time? When have you needed to call upon God's steadfast love and protection? How can you pray in such a situation, using one of these metaphors? Here is a good instance in which a biblical metaphor might inspire us to find our own metaphors, ones that speak more directly to our own life-situations. For example, if you live near the sea or enjoy boating, you may like to use "anchor" in prayer-contexts like these.

You may even find that the Psalms can inspire you to fashion your own metaphors for God. Ellyn Sanna, in *Touching God: Experiencing Metaphors for the Divine,* sees implied, in Psalm 104's references to God making grass grow and watering the trees, a metaphor for God as gardener.

God's Saving Acts as Metaphors for Our Lives

The central event of our Christian tradition is the paschal mystery: Christ's passion, death, and resurrection, through which we have been freed from captivity to sin and death. In the Hebrew Scriptures the event that prefigures Christ's work of redemption is the Exodus event—God's freeing of the chosen people from captivity in Egypt. The Gospels underscore the connection between Exodus and Easter by situating Jesus' passion and death during the Passover feast, in which the Jews commemorate their liberation from bondage in Egypt. This saving event, along with other instances in which God rescued Israel from its enemies, is recalled in a number of psalms that commemorate God's intervention in history on behalf of God's people.

Captivity-to-freedom and death-to-life are paradigms of many events in our own lives. As Christians, we often refer to them as "Good-Friday-to-Easter" events. We can read the "historical" psalms (see especially the lengthy

Psalm 105) to recall and celebrate God's liberation of our ancestors in the faith; at the same time we can also pray with these psalms, or with the relevant parts of them, by interpreting these saving events as metaphors for God's working in our lives. In this way our lives become a microcosm of the great span of salvation history.

Not unexpectedly, *Egypt* becomes a psalmic metaphor for captivity. The sojourn of the Hebrew people in Egypt lasted for four centuries. It began around 1700 BC, when the patriarch Jacob sent his sons to Egypt to obtain food during a famine, at the time when his youngest son, Joseph, whom his brothers had sold into slavery, flourished as the Pharaoh's prime minister. After Joseph's death a new person came to power, so that for about half of their time in Egypt the Hebrews were enslaved in forced labor for the Pharaoh's construction projects. Eventually God chose Moses to lead the people out of Egypt, and thus the Christian tradition honors Moses as a "type" or forerunner of Jesus, who came to free us from sin.

Psalm 80, composed at a low point in Israel's history—a time of harsh trial and brutal invasion, as Pope John Paul II pointed out—begs for the return of God's favor and reminds God of his help in the past:

> You brought a vine out of Egypt;
>> you dispersed the nations and planted it.
> You prepared the ground for it. . . .   (vv. 9-10a)

From what "Egypt" did God rescue me in order to plant my vine? What Egypt held me captive—what insecurities, faults, addictions, unhealthy relationships? How else did God "prepare the ground"—how did God clear my life—in order to plant and let flourish the vine of my right relationship with him so that it might bear fruit in the world?

Psalm 81 summons the people to proper worship of God their savior. In this psalm it is now time for God to remind Israel of his past favors as he says:

> "From your shoulders I lifted the burden;
> I freed the load from your hands.
> You cried out in distress and I saved you;
>   concealed in the storm cloud, I answered."
>
> (vv. 7-8b, NdF)

These verses recall Israel's rescue from forced labor in Egypt and the theophany on Mount Sinai, when the people, seeing the mountain wreathed in thunderclouds and lightning, realized that the Lord was present there. But what do such figures of speech mean to me personally?

Sometimes God speaks to me from the darkest point in my life. From what "storm cloud" in my life did God speak to me? God frees my shoulders from my burdens if I call on God's name. Indeed, God may be concealed in the storm clouds of my life; that very storm cloud may be something I actually come to recognize as God's saving word spoken to me.

In the sixth century BC the lengthy period of Israel's exile and captivity in the kingdom of Babylon came to an end through an edict of Cyrus, King of Persia, who allowed the people to return home. This event is celebrated in Psalm 126:

> When the Lord brought home the captives to Zion,
>   we seemed to be dreaming.
> Our mouths were filled with laughter
>   and our tongues with songs of joy. . . .
> The Lord has indeed done great deeds for us,
>   and we are overflowing with joy. (vv. 1-2a, 3)

When I can put myself in Israel's place—when I can say that the Lord delivered *me* from captivity and can celebrate the "great deeds" the Lord has done for *me*—then I will truly see how my own little life is a microcosm of God's saving work down through all the ages. God's interventions to save Israel from its captors are types or foreshadowings of the great saving act of Christ into which are subsumed the individual gestures of salvation that God works in each of our lives. The psalmist's invaluable legacy to us is these prayer-poems with which we can recall and celebrate these historic saving events as if they sang of our personal salvation.

This chapter has by no means presented an exhaustive discussion of the metaphorical potential of the Psalms. It will, I hope, launch you on your own poetic and prayerful journey through the Psalms by the examples it has provided to guide you in using metaphors from the Psalms and in finding your own metaphors through which you can enrich your conversations with God and your meditations upon God's workings in your life.

Chapter 4

The Psalms and the Liturgy

"We are God's people, the sheep of his flock"

WE have seen how God, in his everlasting love, delivered our ancestors in the faith from captivity in Egypt. This saving act was bound up with a covenant between the Lord and the Hebrew people, whereby the former slaves in Egypt became the nation of Israel, God's chosen people. God promised them, "You shall be my treasured possession out of all the peoples . . . a priestly kingdom and a holy nation" (Ex 19:5-6). Much later the prophet Ezekiel foretold a new and everlasting covenant: "You shall be my people, and I will be your God" (Ez 36:28).

After this new covenant had been sealed with the blood of Christ in his act of redemption on the cross, St. Paul used the metaphor of the body and its members to describe God's people and thereby gave us the term *Body of Christ:*

> For just as the body is one and has many members, and all the members of the body, though many, are one body, so it is with Christ. For in the one Spirit we were all baptized into one body . . . and we were all made to drink of one Spirit.
>
> Now you are the body of Christ and individually members of it. (1 Cor 12:12-13, 27)

We are Christ's body; we are the people of God. We are not a group of individuals who happen somehow to be casually linked to one another through the coincidence of worshiping in the same church. The term *people of God* is no mere figure of speech but a living reality, the reality through which God has chosen to save us.

For a long time awareness of the community dimension of our relationship with God had been lost and the individual's personal relationship with God exclusively emphasized. The Second Vatican Council revived the concept of the church as community and reminded us that we are not simply individual worshipers in a church but members of a community called the people of God. *Lumen Gentium,* the Second Vatican Council's Constitution on the Church, tells us:

> God, however, does not make [people] holy and save them merely as individuals, without bond or link between one another. Rather has it pleased Him to bring [humans] together as one people, a people which acknowledges Him in truth and serves Him in holiness. (# 9)

A life-giving personal relationship with God cannot be nurtured, then, cannot thrive or, indeed, really exist, unless we participate in the community's relationship with God. God's saving deeds belong not only to the individual but to everyone in God's community; they touch everyone's lives. Again, St. Paul says, "If one member suffers, all suffer together with it; if one member is honored, all rejoice together with it" (1 Cor 12:26).

When we are in distress, we bring our need to God before the community so that the community can help us pray. When we praise God for God's favors, we do so publicly so that the community may join in the rejoicing.

A balance between our personal prayer life and our worship in the community is of vital importance, then, if we wish to deepen our relationship with God. Achieving such a balance should be neither daunting nor difficult for us. The Psalms can be our key.

The Psalms: Key to Integrating Personal and Communal Prayer

If you have ever been moved or inspired to use the words of a favorite hymn, or a favorite prayer from the liturgy, as a private prayer, then, even though you may not be aware of it, you are already familiar with integrating your communal with your personal prayer and letting the one nourish the other. The Psalms may well already be among the prayers and hymns that play this role in your prayer life for, perhaps without your realizing it, you have become good friends with many of them through your participation in liturgical worship. Think, for example, of some of our most popular hymns: "A mighty fortress is our God" (Ps 46); "All people that on earth do dwell" (Ps 100); "Yahweh, I know you are near" (Ps 139); "On eagle's wings" (Ps 91); "Loving and forgiving" (Ps 103); "The cry of the poor" (Ps 34). The Psalms, then, should be no strangers to you!

The balance between the personal and the communal is an integral feature of the Psalms:

Set me free from my prison,
   so that I may praise your name.
Then the righteous will assemble around me
   because of your great generosity to me. (Ps 142)

May your saving power, O God, raise me up . . .
I will praise the name of God with a song . . .
Let the poor see this and rejoice;
   let those who seek God take heart. (Ps 69)

When we pray this way, our gift to the community is more than the gift of inviting them to share in our rejoicing; it is also the gift of hope. "The poor [will] see this and rejoice" not only on my behalf but also on their own, because what God did for me God can do for my neighbor if he or she is open to God's saving grace. My prayer of thanksgiving in their presence may be the means of bringing about that openness in that person. In the same way, what God did for me may in itself benefit my neighbor: think of those "wounded healers" who started their ministry after they experienced their own profound psychological or spiritual healing from God.

Our personal prayer and the worship we offer in the community, then, should have a good deal to offer each other. Let's look at some ways of letting the prayers of our liturgical worship enrich our personal prayer routine.

Each week the Responsorial Psalm in the Sunday Mass brings us into contact with a psalm. This provides us with an ideal opportunity to initiate or to further our prayerful acquaintance with the Psalms. The Responsorial Psalm is so called because it is our response to God's word as spoken to us in the First Reading: it reflects on the theme that this Reading has in common with the Gospel. Keeping that theme in mind (the notes in your Missal or the missalette should be of help here), read through the psalm together with the Readings. Be aware of its role as our voice in our dialogue with God: God speaks to us in the Readings, and the psalm is our reply.

Then, pray through the psalm slowly, meditating on the meaning of each line. You may find a line or verse that is particularly meaningful to you; if so, pause at this line, repeat it over and over in your heart, letting God speak to you through it. At some point you may wish to look up the entire psalm in the Bible and pray it in one of these ways, since the Responsorial Psalm usually uses only extracts and rarely an entire psalm.

The Liturgy of the Hours: Prayer of God's People

To pray the Psalms in the Liturgy of the Hours is to follow the great liturgical prayer tradition of Jesus and his church. The Liturgy of the Hours is a collection of the biblical psalms and canticles, along with readings, intercessions, and other prayers, prayed at certain times or "hours" of the day. Each "hour" is arranged in a regular sequence of psalms, readings, and so forth—I will explain the structure of the two most important hours below. An older and perhaps more familiar name for the Liturgy of the Hours is the Divine Office or (from the book that contained it) the Breviary. Until the reforms of Vatican II, this prayer had long been regarded—erroneously—as the exclusive preserve of the clergy.

As its name suggests, the chief purpose of the Liturgy of the Hours is to consecrate time to God. The Second Vatican Council's Constitution on the Liturgy points out that this prayer, rooted in ancient Christian tradition, is "devised so that the whole course of the day and night is made holy by the praises of God" (#84). When Jesus, the Word of God, took on human nature and pitched his tent among us, he "introduced into this earthly exile that hymn which is sung throughout all ages in the halls of heaven" (#83). Jesus urged us to pray unceasingly, and when we pray the Liturgy of the Hours we are truly praising God in the company of Christ and his Body (#84).

In one form or another, the Liturgy of the Hours has been part of Christian worship from the earliest times. The first Christians were Jews, and thus, according to Jewish custom, they offered up certain prayers at regular times during the day. A third-century writer named Hippolytus observed that the meaning of the "prayer of the hours" is the paschal mystery. Each prayer hour, he said, participates in its own way in Christ's redeeming work: for example, at the third hour Christ was nailed to the cross; at the sixth hour began the "great darkness" and so Christians pray in union with the cross; the ninth hour commemorates the flow of blood and water from the side of Christ, Christ's sleep of death, and his resurrection.

Parallel with the development of the Liturgy of the Hours in the regular centers of Christian life, the desert communities were organizing their own regular hours of common prayer. The eventual outcome was two systems of "prayer of the hours," that prayed in towns—called the Cathedral Office—and that prayed by the desert communities of monks, or the Monastic Office. The Cathedral Office, a regular, popular parish service, was more suited to the "secular life" than was the more demanding Monastic Office. It was prayed by priests and lay people alike; thus the Liturgy of the Hours has not always belonged exclusively to the clergy, and there is precedent for the Vatican II reforms that restored it to the laity. It was when people's lifestyles no longer permitted this regular church-going, and when the average person was less and less likely to understand the Latin in which the Office was prayed, that the Divine Office became exclusively the prayer of the clergy.

In recent times it became obvious that the Divine Office in its then-existing form was too cumbersome for the busy lives of modern clergy. What should have been a prayer to sanctify time turned into a burdensome chore that had to be completed by midnight, under pain of mortal sin. And so the Fathers of the Second Vatican Council initiated reforms that simplified the Office. The chief points of the reform were these:

1. The Office—now renamed the Liturgy of the Hours—was to be prayed in the vernacular, not in Latin.

2. The number of the hours was reduced, with Matins (which, in theory, had been a night office) replaced by an Office of Readings to be said at any time, Prime

deleted, and three "Lesser Hours" replaced by Midday Prayer.

3. The 150 Psalms were spread over a four-week cycle instead of having to be prayed all within one week.

4. The laity were to be encouraged to pray the Liturgy of the Hours and to be instructed in praying the chief hours of Lauds (Morning Prayer) and Vespers (Evening Prayer). Moreover, the laity were to be encouraged to celebrate the Liturgy of the Hours not only in church but wherever and for whatever reason they are gathered together in groups, as well as within their own families. In his Apostolic Constitution *Laudis Canticum* of November 1970 promulgating the revised Office Pope Paul VI said:

> Now that the prayer of holy Church has been reformed and entirely revised in keeping with its very ancient tradition and in the light of the needs of our day, it is to be hoped above all that the liturgy of the hours may pervade and penetrate the whole of Christian prayer, giving it life, direction, and expression and effectively nourishing the spiritual life of the people of God.
>
> We have, therefore, every confidence that an appreciation of the prayer "without ceasing" that our Lord Jesus Christ commanded will take on new life. . . . The very celebration of the liturgy of the hours, especially when a community gathered for this purpose expresses the genuine

nature of the praying Church, stands as a wonderful sign of that Church.

The Pope went on to say:

Christian prayer above all is the prayer of the whole human community, which Christ joins to himself. Everyone shares in this prayer, which is proper to the one Body as it offers prayers that give expression to the voice of Christ's beloved Bride, to the hopes and desires of the whole Christian people, and to supplications and petitions for the needs of all humanity.

Thus here, at the very outset of the reform, we find the emphasis on the Liturgy of the Hours as prayer of the Christian community. This communal aspect is underscored in a special way by the fact that, unlike the Mass, the Liturgy of the Hours does not require an ordained minister to preside over it. As liturgical scholar Fr. A. M. Roguet, OP, points out in his "Commentary on the Renewed Liturgy of the Hours," any group of lay people, or even an individual lay person, "if they celebrate the Liturgy of the Hours, . . . are truly praying the prayer of the Church with Christ, and their celebration is 'liturgical' in the fullest sense of the word" (p. 96).*

And vital is the potential of the Liturgy of the Hours for enriching our personal prayer life. Fr. Roguet observes, "The Liturgy of the Hours should nourish our *prayer*. The psalms, said calmly and with attention, renew our awareness of God. They accustom us to

---

* In *The Liturgy of the Hours: The General Instruction with Commentary* (Collegeville, MN: Liturgical Press, 1971).

turning to him, to looking to him, to putting all our hope, all our confidence, the whole of our life in him" (p. 138).

The Psalms not only form the backbone of the Liturgy of the Hours—they also serve to ensure that this prayer is communal prayer, even when prayed in private. The *General Instruction on the Liturgy of the Hours* reminds us that when we pray the psalms in the Liturgy of the Hours we do not do so in our own name but in the name of the entire Body of Christ—in fact, we pray them in the person of Christ himself (#108). This is important to remember if, when praying the Liturgy of the Hours, we find ourselves singing a psalm that doesn't accord with our mood at the moment. As Dr. Joseph Gelineau writes in his Introduction to the Grail translation of the Psalms, do not those who pray the Liturgy of the Hours realize "that they stand before God in the company of the whole of mankind? Their prayer is that of the whole Church and it only reaches the Father through the voice of Christ the Mediator. The psalms compel us to voice all the prayers of the people of God and of their Head; they force us to widen our hearts to the full dimensions of the redemption."

Praying the Psalms in the Liturgy of the Hours ensures that we pray with and through Christ. The Fathers of the church, following the Lord's declaration in Luke 24:44 that "everything written about me in the law of Moses, the prophets, and the psalms must be fulfilled," interpreted the entire Psalter as a prophecy about Christ. The Fathers heard in the Psalms "the voice of

Christ crying out to the Father or of the Father conversing with the Son," says the *General Instruction* (#109). Thus when we pray the Liturgy of the Hours we follow Christ's invitation to pray in his name and thereby join with the church in continuing his eternal prayer.

How the Liturgy of the Hours is organized

The Second Vatican Council's Constitution on the Sacred Liturgy states, "By the venerable tradition of the universal Church, Lauds as morning prayer and Vespers as evening prayer are the two hinges on which the daily Office turns; hence they are to be considered as the chief Hours and are to be celebrated as such" (#89 a). As we have seen, the Council wished that the laity be encouraged to pray Lauds and Vespers. These two hours celebrate the rising and the setting of the sun, to be sure—but not only that. In praying Lauds the church celebrates the resurrection of Christ, "the rising sun," symbolized by the dawn. Vespers corresponds to the setting of the sun, the hour of the evening sacrifice and prayer of thanksgiving for the gifts received during the day.

Lauds and Vespers have parallel structures, which make them relatively easy to follow if you wish to pray them. A diagram showing the structure of the two hours is given in Fig. 1, p. 78, and following that, an explanation of each component.

Lauds	Vespers

Introductory verse: "O God, come to my assistance . . ."
Doxology: "Glory to the Father…"

Hymn suitable to the hour or the feast

Lauds	Vespers
Antiphon	Antiphon
Psalm	Psalm
Psalm-prayer	Psalm-prayer
Antiphon	Antiphon
OT Canticle	Psalm
	Psalm-prayer
Antiphon	Antiphon
Psalm	NT Canticle
Psalm-prayer	

Scripture Reading
(Homily or Reflection)
Responsory

Antiphon
Gospel Canticle:

Lauds	Vespers
Canticle of Zechariah	Canticle of Mary
(Benedictus)	(Magnificat)

Intercessions
Lord's Prayer
Concluding Prayer
Dismissal

Fig. 1

The components of the Hours

Psalms. It can't be said often enough: the Psalms are the backbone of the Liturgy of the Hours. The Psalms are prayers from the Hebrew Scriptures, born of a particular culture. Traditionally the church gives the psalms and canticles in the Liturgy of the Hours a Christian coloring by concluding each with the Doxology.* The Liturgy of the Hours incorporates three further aids in understanding the psalms and making them truly Christian prayer:

1. **Antiphons.** Each psalm and each canticle is preceded and followed (after the Doxology) by a brief verse called an antiphon. The antiphon can personalize the psalm; can highlight a particular aspect of it; can highlight its Christian interpretation, which is especially true of the antiphons for certain feasts. Many of the antiphons that have an ancient history in the church are beautiful literary or poetic compositions in their own right and have been set to music by the great composers, especially in the sixteenth century.

2. **Psalm-prayers.** It was an ancient custom for the monks, after they had sung a psalm, to remain for some moments in silent prayer, after which the presider prayed a collect to sum up the main theme of the psalm. The church still uses some of these ancient psalm-prayers, along with other more recent ones. The psalm-prayer is prayed at the conclusion of the psalm (after the Doxology and antiphon), and its

---

* "Glory to the Father, and to the Son, and to the Holy Spirit, as it was in the beginning, is now, and will be forever. Amen."

function is to sum up the psalm and give it a Christian interpretation.

3. **Headings before each psalm.** The heading consists of a title that states what the psalm is about, just as any poem or song has a title, and a phrase from the New Testament or a church Father that casts the psalm in the light of Christian revelation (or, we might say, brings out its christological aspect). These headings are not meant to be sung or read out loud.

Canticles from the Hebrew Scriptures or the New Testament. The canticles really are psalms or sacred poetry preserved in Scripture in places other than the Book of Psalms. They include:

From the Hebrew Scriptures: Hannah's canticle from 1 Samuel in which Hannah gives thanks for the birth of her son Samuel (it is very similar to Mary's *Magnificat*); the song of the Exodus that Moses and the people sang when God led them out of Egypt; a prayer for wisdom from the Book of Wisdom; and many canticles from the Book of Isaiah, which contains some of the most beautiful poetry in Scripture.

From the New Testament: several from the writings of St. Paul, in which he appears to be quoting some early Christian hymns; several hymns from the Book of Revelation.

Reading. Readings from Scripture are an important element in the Liturgy of the Hours, just as they were an important part of Christian prayer services from the earliest times. In Lauds and Vespers a short or long reading is given after the psalmody. The *General Instruction* tells us that the reading of Scripture in the liturgy "is to have special importance for all Christians . . . because [it] is not the result of individual choice of devotion but is the planned decision of the Church itself" (#140).

The readings are followed by a **Responsory,** which is meant to be a brief meditative prayer responding to the reading that has just been heard.

The two **Gospel Canticles** take special pride of place in Morning and Evening Prayer. These are the major "psalms" to have been preserved in the New Testament. At Lauds the Canticle of Zechariah, or *Benedictus,* is prayed, with its appropriate reference to Christ as "the dawn from on high" (Luke 1:78), and at Vespers the Canticle of Mary or *Magnificat.* The *General Instruction* prescribes that these canticles "be treated with the same solemnity and dignity as are customary at the proclamation of the gospel itself" (#138).

The **Prayers** are similar in structure to the Prayers of the Faithful at Mass. At Lauds the prayers consecrate the day to God; at Vespers they are intercessory prayers. St. Paul exhorts us to offer "supplications, prayers, intercessions, and thanksgiving . . . for everyone . . . so that we may lead a quiet and peaceable life in all godliness and dignity. This is right and is acceptable in the sight of God our Savior, who desires everyone to be saved and to come to the knowledge of the truth" (1 Tim 2:1-4; cf. *General Instruction* # 179), and the church Fathers often took this to mean that such prayers should be offered in the morning and evening.

The Prayers are followed by the **Lord's Prayer** and then by a brief **Concluding Prayer.** On Sundays, solemnities, feasts, and memorials, as well as on the weekdays of Advent, the Christmas season, Lent, and the Easter season, the concluding prayer is the same as the collect or opening prayer for the Mass of the day.

Hymns have always had an important place in the Liturgy of the Hours. They are intended to be truly "popular" in that they draw the people into the prayer and express the character of the hour or of the feast more directly than do other parts of the liturgy. At Lauds and Vespers the hymn immediately follows the Introductory Verse and Doxology.

How to begin

If you've never prayed the Liturgy of the Hours, it may take some practice, but once you accustom yourself to its rhythms, you will be richly rewarded by your participation in this ancient and timeless prayer of the church. Short, user-friendly editions have been produced precisely with busy people in mind (see the Resource List at the back of the book). Don't feel that you have to plunge right in by committing yourself to praying both the morning and the evening hours, or even to praying any individual hour in its entirety. Even praying only one of the hours, or choosing one of the psalms from the hour and praying or meditating on it in one of the ways suggested earlier in the chapter for the Responsorial Psalm of the Mass, will suffice to give you a flavor of the Liturgy of the Hours as well as the opportunity to join in the prayer of the universal church.

This universal dimension is the essential characteristic of the Liturgy of the Hours: in praying it we are praying with and for the community, joining with our neighbor in the pew at Sunday Mass as well as with Catholics on the other side of the world totally unknown to us. This is good to remember when we find we are praying a psalm that doesn't reflect our personal thoughts or feelings at the time. On such occasions we can, if we wish, pray such a psalm on behalf of another person as if we were that person. We can be their voice, their soul before God; we can praise or thank God for a favor God has shown them, or appeal to God in their need. In this way we take into ourselves, and represent to God, the distress of a loved one in trouble, the gratitude of a friend who has enjoyed some success, or the sorrow of an anonymous, suffering individual who has no one else to pray for them.

The possibilities for adapting the format of the Liturgy of the Hours for your own prayer routine are virtually endless. Once you cultivate the habit of thinking of this Prayer as a rich treasure chest of spirituality that you can "dip into," you will surely develop your own ways of letting its spirit of universality or its psalm-prayer-reading-intercession rhythm strengthen your personal prayer routine.

As I suggested above, if you haven't the time to pray the entire hour, you may wish to choose one or two from the psalms and canticles. You can also substitute another reading for the Scripture reading given; an obvious choice would be one of the readings from the Mass of the day. Or if—during Lent, for example—you are working your way through a book of brief meditations or have arranged a Scripture-reading program for yourself, you can use these during your Morning or Evening Prayer. Lives of the Saints that are historically based rather than legendary in spirit are also suitable.

For the Prayers you may insert your prayers for a personal intention instead of or in addition to the prayers in the book. You may even find that one of the prayer intentions in the book can itself provide material for a brief meditation, a starting point from which to speak to God in your own words.

If you regularly engage in a prayer routine such as Prayer of Quiet or Centering Prayer, a psalm from Lauds or Vespers can be prayed as a means of centering down or of ending your prayer, or both; or a short phrase from one of the psalms or the canticle can be used as your mantra.

When you attend Mass and arrive at church sufficiently early, praying parts of the Liturgy of the Hours is an excellent way to prepare for celebrating the Eucharist. You may wish to pray one of the praise psalms for thanksgiving after Communion.

Psalms and the Sacrament of Penance

Finally, another important area of interaction between our personal and communal or liturgical prayer that can be nourished by the Psalms is the Sacrament of Penance. We can pray psalms to give words to our preparation and thanksgiving for the sacrament, and as our act of contrition.

Preparation. As frail human beings it sometimes happens that we approach this sacrament with some trepidation. Psalm 103—

> Bless the Lord, O my soul;
>> my entire being, bless his holy name (v. 1)

—puts before us a God who is Pure Love; a God who "removes our transgressions from us," a God whom we need not fear to approach to confess our sins. This beautiful psalm can also be prayed as thanksgiving after celebrating the sacrament.

Sometimes we feel overwhelmed by our seeming inability to overcome temptation, and if we wish to convey this to God in prayer, Psalm 86, a psalm of distress, can help with the words. It addresses a God of mercy, and we can use the references to the enemies who seek our life as metaphors for those things, external but especially internal, that cause us to fall into sin.

Act of Contrition. Psalm 51, the greatest of all penitential psalms, known as the *Miserere* because of its first Latin word—

> Have mercy on me, O God,
>> in accord with your kindness;
> in your abundant compassion
>> wipe away my offenses (v. 1)

—is attributed to King David when he expressed remorse for his adultery with Bathsheba, wife of his friend Uriah. The church prescribes the use of this psalm

in Morning Prayer every Friday, in commemoration of
the day on which Jesus died for our sins; it is also prayed
frequently during Lent. As Pope John Paul II observed,
Psalm 51 is "a hymn raised to the merciful God by the
repentant sinner," recognizing above all that sin corrodes
our relationship with God.

Psalm 130, another famous penitential psalm, was
long prayed in Christian tradition on behalf of the dead,
but we may well appropriate its words for our own spirit of remorse leading to hope in the God in whom there
is kindness and fullness of redemption. Familiar in
Christian tradition as the *De profundis,* it begins:

>Out of the depths I cry to you, O Lord;
>O Lord, hear my voice. (vv. 1-2a)

Thanksgiving. Psalm 32—

>Blessed is the one whose offense is forgiven,
>whose sin is erased (v. 1)

—verbalizes the relief felt by the penitent on openly con-
fessing his or her sin to God. It also offers God's promise
to respect our human freedom: this is a God who
"instructs us and guides us in the way we should go,"
not a God who forces us, as if we were animals to be led
about bridled.

We do well to remember that the Sacrament of
Penance isn't simply a one-on-one transaction between
us—the penitent—and God, but also marks our reconcil-
iation with the church community, the people of God of
whom we are a part. In Psalm 100, the great thanksgiving psalm that reminds us that we are the flock that God

shepherds, we give thanks to God as part of that community of worshipers and not merely as private individuals.

This chapter has presented an extensive but by no means exhaustive list of suggestions for how to pray the Psalms in liturgical prayer. As you deepen your acquaintance with the Psalms as they function in the liturgy you will undoubtedly discover additional ways, as well, of using them to integrate your communal with your personal prayer. When we pray this way we need never feel alone; we are always a part of God's people and thus members of Christ himself.

Chapter 5

The Psalms and Eucharistic Spirituality

"I will give thanks to your name"

THE Second Letter of Peter tells us, "With the Lord one day is like a thousand years, and a thousand years are like one day" (3:8). As children we may have experienced this counsel as little more than a frustrating corrective to our natural impatience. With the gaining of maturity, however, perhaps our frustration gave way to consolation as we came to realize that Peter is saying that God's time scale is not ours: God would, indeed, hear our prayers and help us in what God's divine wisdom deemed to be the *right* time. Yet, Peter is also teaching a far more profound lesson here, one that has to do not so much with God's wisdom as with God's compassion and love.

We are accustomed to measuring events in terms of time. First Event A happened, then Event B happened after that. This is how our finite minds grasp things—as a series of chronological events, some of which may have caused or given rise to others. But we are also fortunate to be living in an age when developments in scientific knowledge have given us a more sophisticated understanding of how the universe works, particularly with regard to the relativity of time, and this new understanding can only serve to enrich our perception of God and how God works.

God—who is compassion and love—is eternal. God exists outside of time. God's saving help, which flows from divine compassion and love, also exists outside of time: it is *one* act, *one* event, but its effects, as experienced by us, are spread out in time. The event itself, however, is timeless—it transcends time.

How do we participate in this? What direct meaning does God's timelessness have for our own lives and for our relationship with God? And how can the Psalms support and nourish this relationship?

First, let us go back to the big saving event in Jewish history: the Exodus—the deliverance of the people of Israel, our ancestors in the faith, from bondage under the pharaohs of Egypt. The Passover feast, the ritual meal celebrated by the Jews, is a memorial of that saving event.

Memorial is a very central concept in Jewish thinking. It does not simply mean "remembering": it means reliving the event; re*actual*izing it in such a way that the effects, the fruits of that event, are brought into the present time. This is what the Passover celebration does: it relives the original Exodus event so that its effects are made present in the here and now for those who are celebrating it.

We have already seen that Christian tradition reveres many people and events in the Hebrew Scriptures as types, or prefigurations, of the life and work of Christ.

The Exodus event, the release from Egyptian bondage, prefigures *the* great saving event of human history: Christ's redemption, the act by which Christ freed us from the captivity of sin. Ancient liturgical tradition acclaims Christ as the "new Moses" who has liberated us from the "Egypt" of our sinful state. Scripture readings and psalms commemorating the Exodus as the core event of Old Testament salvation history, and thus as a "type" of Christ's redemptive act, play a central role in our present-day Easter liturgy. You will note this over and over again if you look at the texts for the Easter liturgy, whether readings, psalms, or antiphons, whether the Vigil Mass, the Sunday Mass, or the Liturgy of the Hours.

Just as the Passover event is a memorial celebration of the Exodus event, so, too, the Eucharist is a memorial celebration of Christ's redemption of humanity. And it is a memorial in the same sense: that is, it does not merely remember this redemptive event, but relives it, re*presents* it—literally, makes it present again, so that the effects of Christ's saving act on the cross are *real*ized—made real—for us, here and now. The very presence of the saving act, and of the body and blood of Christ sacrificed to bring that act about, become reactualized in the liturgy.

Thus, both the Passover and the Eucharist are celebrations that transcend time. They reach beyond time to God's timeless saving help—as manifested in the old and new covenants respectively—and bring it into time, crystallizing in time the effects of the events they celebrate.

God's acts, and therefore Christ's acts, are not limited either by chronological time or by duration; the effect of each act will be realized when God wills it to be realized—and it was the will of God that the effects of Christ's redemption should be realized—made real—whenever we celebrate the Eucharist. The Eucharist, the new Passover, is a personal memorial of Jesus. In the Eucharist Jesus himself, our Savior, is personally present; through the Eucharist the saving effects of his passion and death are made present to us who celebrate it. And when we celebrate the Eucharist we also bring the future into the present by proclaiming Christ's coming again in glory.

How do the Psalms play a role in all this? The Psalms are the prayers that help us to enflesh this eucharistic awareness in our personal prayer life. Many of them are a microcosm of this process of telescoping past, present, and future. They embody in prayer the timeless quality of God's goodness, and insofar as they do this they are our models for eucharistic prayer—that is, prayer centered in the Eucharist, prayer enlivened by our eucharistic faith.

A eucharistic memory is a grateful memory. To have a eucharistic memory means to live in grateful remembrance of God's goodness to us, grateful awareness of how Christ touches and heals us, not only us here and now but people for all time. This grateful awareness enables us to reach out and to be Christ for others: to be agents of his healing work because we, in turn, have experienced his healing. As followers of Christ we are called to be healed and to be healers, and for us to have a eucharistic memory is directly related to that call.

In cultivating this eucharistic memory and developing a prayer life truly centered in the spirit of the Eucharist, the Psalms are our models for prayer. As the Exodus prefigures the Redemption, and as the Passover prefigures the Eucharist, so, too, the Psalms prefigure the eucharistic memory. The Psalms express the complete unity of all the manifestations of God's love. In Psalm 85 we pray:

> Show us, O LORD, your kindness
> and grant us your salvation. (v. 8)

The kindness of the Lord that we pray for—the Hebrew word for "kindness," *hesed*, also means "saving help" and "mercy"—is the same kindness that brought Israel out of Egypt; the same saving help that rescued Israel from its enemies later in its history as well. It is, as Pope John Paul II reminded us, God's "generous fidelity" toward the people of the covenant. What we are really praying for is, "Make the effects of your saving help manifest in time again; make it present in our lives, here and now."

Psalm 13 is an excellent example of the telescoping of past, present, and future. It begins,

> How long, O LORD—will you forget me forever?
> How long will you hide your face from me? (v. 2)

The psalmist pours out his sorrow and anguish and begs for God's saving help. Yet, the psalm ends with an expression of trust in God's kindness and the promise,

> I will sing to the LORD
> because he has been good to me. (v. 7)

These are ambiguous lines. Are they recalling God's help in the past or anticipating God's future help in the present situation? Perhaps both. It is interesting to note that composers during the Renaissance set to music an excerpt from this psalm, "enlighten my eyes, lest I sleep in death, lest my enemy say, 'I have defeated him' " (vv. 4b-5a), addressing it to Jesus (*O bone Jesu*, "O good Jesus")—an example of how our tradition has "christianized" the Psalms by interpreting them in terms of Jesus or, as in this case, addressing them to him.

Many of the Psalms follow the pattern of bringing past, present, and future together by recalling God's help in the past, stating the present situation, and anticipating God's saving help. In chapter 2 we saw a classic psalm in this vein, Psalm 22, "My God, my God, why have you forsaken me?" which starts in desolation and ends with the certainty of deliverance and the anticipation of how I will praise and thank God.

How *does* the psalmist praise and thank God? He thanks God "in the great assembly"—in other words, before the entire community. The psalmist thanks God publicly, and he does this so that the community may rejoice with him. In speaking of the communal dimension of our prayer in chapter 4, we saw how proclaiming God's goodness to us in public can be a gift of hope to people; in this way we start to act as signs, sacraments, of God's healing. The Gospel of Mark tells the story of Jesus healing the Gerasene demoniac. After he is healed the man begs Jesus to allow him to accompany Jesus.

"But Jesus refused, and said to him, 'Go home to your friends, and tell them how much the Lord has done for you, and what mercy he has shown you'" (5:19). It is no accident that the church prescribes this as one of the Gospels for Thanksgiving Day In telling our friends "how much the Lord has done for" us, we are doing nothing more or less than following the command of Jesus.

The Scriptures are full of references to the Lord who "keeps faith forever" (cf. Psalm 146). God's faith, his fidelity, is eternal. We experience its effects in time, and as we experience it our own faith in God is nourished; our remembrance of God's past goodness inspires our faith that God is supporting us at the present time and will help and support us in the future. To pray with psalm-faith means that we pray with an attitude that is a grateful remembering of God's past help and, *at the same time,* confidence in God's present and future help. It is to pray with awareness that "the Lord keeps faith forever." When we express this faith in our prayer we have to do so chronologically: now we recall the past, now we state the present, now we look to the future—that is simply the way our human language works. But when we get beyond language to that part of ourselves where this faith actually lives within us, then gratitude for the past and confidence in the present and future all blend into one attitude of faith: an attitude that is at once psalm-faith and eucharistic faith.

God's loving care for us stretches all through time. It transcends and lasts beyond our earthly death to our life after that. God's loving care is *one* act, *one* event whose effects we experience at different points in time. When we pray for our friends and loved ones we participate in God's loving care for them; God's gift to us is to allow us to participate in this way in his care for our loved ones. And when we pray out of love for people, we share in God's timelessness.

If we truly love someone, we love that person in their entirety; that means we love them as they are now and as they were in the past, even before we knew them. To the extent that we love that person as they were in the past, the prayers we pray out of love for them encompass their past and thus may have helped them even at a time "before" we actually knew the person concerned.

A German proverb says, "Those who live in the Lord never see each other for the last time." When we develop the habit of praying with psalm-faith, with the eucharistic memory that telescopes past, present, and future into one eternal event, we begin really to believe this, not because we have been told that we will meet our loved ones again in heaven, but because there develops within us the inner conviction of the truth of this statement. When we really live in the Lord, when we really pray in the spirit of the Eucharist and with the psalm-faith in which grateful memory of God's past action informs confidence in God's action in present and future, then those we love are forever present to us, and the concept of the Communion of Saints truly becomes for us a living reality. In this way we share in a divine quality, because God thus allows our love to transcend the limits of time—in the words of the Second Letter of Peter, to transform one "today" into a thousand yesterdays.

Chapter 6

"Who's Who" in the Psalms

THIS chapter presents a sort of glossary of unfamiliar names and terms in the Psalms. Our praying of the Psalms will be considerably deepened if we can truly enter the minds and hearts of our forebears in salvation history who composed and first prayed them, and knowing what these terms meant in the history, culture, and daily life of the people of Israel is indispensable to this process.

The most obvious way of using the glossary is to look up the terms as you encounter them in your reading and praying of the Psalms. In addition, the numbers of the psalms in which each term appears are given after the respective entries, so that if you wish, you can first read an entry in the glossary and then look it up in the context of the psalm or psalms in which it appears. Be sure also to refer to chapter 3 for explanations of many terms that the psalmists frequently used as metaphors.

Abiram, see Dathan.

Amalek, see Ammon.

Ammon. The Ammonites and Amalekites were long-standing foes of Israel. The Amalekites, a fierce tribe, were defeated by Moses when he stretched out his rod over them. Saul achieved important victories over both tribes. *83*

Assyria, see Midian.

Baal. One of the chief Canaanite gods, a fertility god who died and was resurrected annually. Baal's cult, which featured licentious dances and meals, contrasted with the more morally exacting God of Israel; thus the Israelites were often attracted by, and lapsed into, Baal worship. During the time of Moses they incurred God's anger when they worshiped Baal on a mountain called Peor. *106*

Babylon. A very powerful empire in the ancient world. In the sixth century BC Nebuchadnezzar, the king of Babylon, destroyed Jerusalem and the Temple, took control of Judea, and exiled most of the Jewish people, except the poor, to Babylon. This Babylonian Captivity lasted about half a century until King Cyrus of Persia conquered Babylon and allowed the Jews to return to Jerusalem. The "rivers of Babylon," by which the Israelites sat and wept and refused to sing songs for their captors, were the two great rivers of ancient times, the Tigris and the Euphrates. *87, 137*

Benjamin. One of the Twelve Tribes of Israel. *68, 80*

Canaan. In the Hebrew Scriptures Canaan denoted all the land between the Jordan and the Mediterranean, from Egypt into Syria. Israel's conquest of this Promised

Land took place only gradually, from the time when God promised Abraham a land for his people until the assignment of territories to the Twelve Tribes. A cult practice among the pagan Canaanites was the offering of children to the God Molech by passing them through fire. *106, 135*

Dathan and Abiram took part in a rebellion against Moses and Aaron in the wilderness. In order to show that it was the Lord who had sent Moses, God caused the earth to open and swallow Dathan, Abiram, and their families so that they went alive down to Sheol. *106*

Dragon. A mythological monster, symbol of evil as well as historical foes such as Babylon and Egypt. *91*

Eagle. A bird of prey whose recuperative powers and nurture of its young are among its well-known traits. *103*

Edom. An ancient kingdom that David eventually brought under his control. The Edomites were thought to have descended from Jacob's brother, Esau, so that "Edomites" can sometimes identify anyone not an Israelite. *60, 83, 108, 137*

Endor, see Jabin.

Ephraim. One of the Twelve Tribes of Israel. *60, 78, 80, 108*

Ephrata, or Valley of Rephaim. See Yearim.

Ethiopia. An ancient region bordering on Egypt. Around the ninth century BC the king of Judah defeated aggression by the Ethiopian army. *68, 87*

Gilead. A high area, good for grazing, and claimed by the Israelites. Gilead's hardy trees were renowned for their healing balm. Saul's victory over the Ammonites took place in Gilead. *60, 108*

Hagar, see Ishmael.

Ham. Youngest son of Noah, called "father of Canaan." Because Ham looked upon and did not cover his father's nakedness when he saw him lying drunk, Noah cursed Canaan that it would become the slave of the descendants of his two other sons, Shem and Japheth. One of the sons of Ham was Egypt, and thus Egypt is sometimes referred to as the "land of Ham." *105, 106*

Hermon, Mount. Also called Sirion by the people of the ancient Phoenician city of Sidon. A high, majestic peak at the northern limit of the land conquered by Israel. The snow with which it is covered all year melts down into, and is the principal source of, the river Jordan. *42, 89, 133*

Holy mountain, see Zion.

Horeb. Another name for Mount Sinai, where Moses smote the rock to obtain water for the thirsty Hebrews, and where the people made the golden calf. 106

Horses were a very useful and versatile animal in Old Testament times. They were used for farm work, for hauling, hunting, and in the military. Solomon had thousands of horses in his army. *20, 33*

Ishmael. Son of Abraham and Hagar, his concubine. Like Isaac, Abraham's son by his wife, Sarah, Ishmael was also the ancestor of twelve tribes but, because they were the descendants of the Egyptian-born Hagar, they were considered inferior to the nation of Israel. *83*

Jaar, see Yearim.

Jabin. King of Canaan whose army, led by Sisera, was defeated at the River Kishon, an epoch-making event that ended his twenty-year oppression of Israel. The small town of Endor, near Nazareth, may have been the site of this battle in which the Israelites were led by the valiant Deborah and Barak. *83*

Jacob. The younger son of Isaac and Rebecca. The angel with whom Jacob wrestled in the night gave him the new name of Israel, and he is often regarded as the personification of the nation of Israel as well as being its ancestor. His name, Jacob, is sometimes used to mean the entire nation. *14, 20, 22, 24, 44, 46, 47, 53, 75, 76, 77, 78, 79, 81, 84, 85, 87, 94, 105, 114, 132, 135, 146, 147*

Judah. One of the Twelve Tribes of Israel. *60, 108*

Kadesh. Located on the Sinai Peninsula, the central campsite occupied by Israel during their wanderings in the wilderness, en route to the Promised Land. As it was a wild area of seasonal rains Moses had to send out people to locate adequate water supplies. *29*

Kedar. A region to the east of Palestine, inhabited by Bedouin people whose superior animal flocks and black tents were well known. *120*

Leviathan. A mythical, many-headed sea monster, symbol of evil that is defeated, in the end, through the power of good. *74*

Lot had two sons who became the ancestors of the Moabites and Ammonites respectively. (See also Moab, Ammon.) *83*

Manasseh. One of the Twelve Tribes of Israel. *60, 80, 108*

Massah. A place near Mount Sinai where Moses produced water from a rock by striking it with his rod when the thirsty Israelites were murmuring against God. *95*

Meribah, see Massah. *81, 95, 106*

Meshech. A people founded by Noah's grandson Japheth, they were a merchant nation that inhabited southeast Asia Minor. *120*

Midian. Israel considered its pagan enemies Assyria and Midian to be a scourge sent by God. The Midianites are sometimes identified as "Ishmaelites." The Midianite princes Oreb and Zeëb were slain at the command of the

Israelite leader Gideon during the advance to the River Jordan. Later Gideon himself killed the Midianite kings Zebah and Zalmunna. *83*

Mizar, Hill of. A small hill near Mount Hermon (q.v.). *42*

Moab. An ancient kingdom in the Jordan region, eventually subdued by King David. The Moabites were thought to have descended from the daughters of Lot. An ancestor of Jesus, Ruth, was a Moabite. *60, 83, 108*

Moth. A notorious consumer of clothing, the moth is ubiquitous in the lands in which the events of Scripture took place. *39*

Naphthah. One of the Twelve Tribes of Israel. *68*

Og, see Bashan.

Oil had many uses in Old Testament times, including the anointing of guests as a sign of hospitality. *23, 92, 133*

Ophir. A region in southwest Arabia, renowned for its famous gold. Gold of Ophir adorned Solomon's temple as well as his armor and his throne. *45*

Oreb, see Midian.

Peor, see Baal. *106*

Philistines. Inhabitants of the Mediterranean coast, west of Israel and Judah. Although Israel never permanently conquered them, the Philistines did come under control of and pay heavy tribute to David and Solomon. *60, 83, 87, 108*

Phinehas. Grandson of Aaron and a high priest. He killed an Israelite who was responsible for seducing the Hebrews into the worship of Baal. *106*

Rahab. A mythological dragon, conquered by Yahweh before he created the universe. Rahab is associated with chaos. *89*

River Kishon, see Jabin. *83*

Sheba. A wealthy kingdom in western Arabia whose people enjoyed a reputation as merchants. The Queen of Sheba visited Solomon in order that the two rulers could work out a trade alliance, and she was sumptuously entertained by him. *72*

Shechem. A strategically located city about forty miles north of Jerusalem. Abimelech, son of Gideon, enlisted the help of the people of Shechem in slaying his seventy brothers so that he could rule Shechem, but God cursed Abimelech and the people for this crime by setting them against one another. *60, 108*

Shiloh. An important Israelite town and resting place for the ark. During the war with the Philistines the Ark was captured, but when the Philistines returned the Ark to Israel it was not placed in Shiloh again. *78*

Sihon, see Bashan in chapter 3.

Sirion, see Hermon.

Sisera, see Jabin.

Succoth. A town in the Jordan region. Gideon, the Israelite general, took revenge upon its people when they refused to provide bread for his army in the campaign against the Midianites. *60, 108*

Tabor. A mountain in Galilee, about five miles east of Nazareth. Although not particularly high it is made conspicuous by its isolated position. *89*

Tarshish. The word means "mine" or "refinery." In biblical times the well-known ships of Tarshish plied the Mediterranean and Red Seas, carrying silver and other metals. *48, 72*

Tyre. An ancient, very wealthy seaport of Phoenicia, it symbolized worldly prominence. Relations between the Phoenicians and the Israelites were generally friendly, although the Israelites considered the Phoenician religion a threat. *45, 83, 87*

Viper. A poisonous snake, symbol of evil. *91*

Washing of hands. Part of the purification ceremony to prepare for approaching the altar. It was not permitted for either priests or worshipers to approach the altar unless they had washed in running water. *26*

Yearim, Kiriath-jearim, Jaar. The place in the Valley of Rephaim (or Ephrata) where the Ark of the Lord rested for some twenty years until David took it up to Jerusalem. *132*

Zalmon, Mount. Possibly a peak of the sacred mountain of Samaria, Mount Gerizim. *68*

Zalmunna, see Midian.

Zebah, see Midian.

Zebulun. One of the Twelve Tribes of Israel. *68*

Zeëb, see Midian.

Zion. The name originally referred to the east ridge between two valleys up which early Jerusalem spread. Its rocky nature made it a mighty fortress-stronghold. King David conquered it and made Zion the holy place of the Jews. Thus while the name Zion is sometimes synonymous with Jerusalem itself, it specifically came to refer to the holy mountain, the place of the Temple where the Ark of the Covenant was kept. The association of the holy temple site with this natural fortress-like quality inspired people to call God their rock, refuge, stronghold, or fortress. The Holy of Holies, dwelling-place of the Ark, was prefigured by the portable sanctuary or tent used by the Israelites as a place of worship during their time of wandering in the wilderness. Moses pitched this tent outside the camp, where those who wished to pray and meditate could visit it. *2, 3, 7, 9, 11, 14, 15, 16, 18, 19,*

20, 24, 25, 27, 28, 31, 32, 36, 37, 42, 46, 48, 50, 51, 53, 57, 61, 62, 64, 65, 69, 71, 73, 76, 78, 84, 87, 89, 90, 91, 92, 94, 95, 97, 99, 102, 110, 125, 126, 128, 129, 132, 133, 134, 135, 137, 141, 142, 143, 144, 146, 149

Zoan. Capital of Egypt for a period, and commercially important, Zoan is significant in the Exodus. *76*

Resources for Further Reading

Christian Prayer, the official one-volume edition of the Liturgy of the Hours, with complete texts of Morning and Evening Prayer for the entire year. (Totowa, NJ: Catholic Book Publishing Corp., 1976).

General Instruction on the Liturgy of the Hours, Liturgy Documentary Series 5, rev. ed. (Washington, DC: USCCB, 2002).

Liturgy of the Hours, the official four-volume English edition of the Divine Office that contains the translation of the International Committee on English in the Liturgy approved by the Episcopal Conference of the U.S. and 26 other English-speaking countries (Totowa, NJ: Catholic Book Publishing Corp., 1975/1976).

The Psalms: New Catholic Version (Totowa, NJ: Catholic Book Publishing Corp., 2002).

Shorter Christian Prayer, with Morning and Evening Prayer from the Four-Week Psalter and selected texts for the Seasons and Major Feasts of the year. A user-friendly, portable version of the above. (Totowa, NJ: Catholic Book Publishing Corp., 1988).

Ellyn Sanna, *Touching God: Experiencing Metaphors for the Divine* (Mahwah, NJ: Paulist Press, 2002).

Shirley Darcus Sullivan, *A Companion to the Liturgy of the Hours: Morning and Evening Prayer* (Totowa, NJ: Catholic Book Publishing Corp., 2004).

Additional Titles Published by Resurrection Press, a Catholic Book Publishing Imprint

For a free catalog call 1-800-892-6657

www.catholicbookpublishing.com